Talking About
Wine with Ease

Linda R. Foxworth & Robert W. Wildman, II

Order this book online at www.trafford.com
or email orders@trafford.com

Most Trafford titles are also available at major online book retailers.

Print information available on the last page.

ISBN: 978-1-4907-5886-2 (sc)
ISBN: 978-1-4907-5887-9 (e)

Library of Congress Control Number: 2015906244

Trafford rev. 05/06/2015

Trafford
PUBLISHING®   www.trafford.com
North America & international
toll-free: 1 888 232 4444 (USA & Canada)
fax: 812 355 4082

Talking About Wine with Ease

A brief summary of and
guide to the world
of wine written for those
wishing to quickly
learn to function in social
and business settings
in which wines are served, discussed and
appreciated

Linda R. Foxworth, *Certified Specialist of Wine*

Robert W. Wildman, II,
Certified Specialist of Wine

Contents

DEDICATIONS

For Dixie. Thank you for your encouragement, advice and wicked sense of humor.

--Linda R. Foxworth

This book is dedicated to my grandmother, Fay Keller Wildman Digby, who was ever grateful for wine in its Sacramental, as well as its other manifestations. I would also like to acknowledge the editorial and graphic design contributions of Linda D. Wildman.

--Robert W. Wildman, II

CHAPTER 1

INTRODUCTION AND
WINE BASICS

Congratulations! You have achieved or are achieving a responsible position in life. You have important duties and a voice in organizational meetings. You are also asked to entertain colleagues, bosses and affluent clients.

Of course, you've been preparing yourself for this new role for years. You took the right courses to qualify for advancement in this industry. You also took such electives as art and music appreciation to make sure that you were ready for the social aspects of this job. But another part of this life, wine knowledge, has, in all probability, been so far left out of your education. After all, few of us grew up in an environment in which fine wines were routinely served and discussed. There are, for obvious reasons, no undergraduate survey courses on wine.

This little book seeks to remediate this small gap in your broadly-defined education. It is hoped that this brief resource, in conjunction with your own then more finely-tuned observations, will help you in rather immediately functioning successfully in the world of entertaining with wine.

Features of this Work

Pronunciation guide. To help you learn to rapidly function in this area, we are presenting a simplified guide to pronouncing wine-related terms which relies upon common English words and obvious nonsense syllables. For example, the best known wine producing area of France is Bordeaux. While an encyclopedia would guide you to say this name as "bawr doh," we opt for the more intuitive "bore dough." For the sake of brevity, each non-English word will be "pronounced out" only once, even if that same word recurs in subsequent names presented.

Talking points. These are standard, safe comments which are frequently used by people who are knowledgeable about wines. Employed cautiously, your saying them yourself makes you appear to be an insider in this area of study and jazzes up your conversations at social functions.

Things to remember. These are the primary pieces of information about each country/chapter which the authors believe should most definitely be remembered

Overview not a handbook. We hope you will find this little book worthy of being read in its entirety. For the sake of brevity, information presented in one chapter is not repeated in other chapters to which it is also relevant.

Maps. All outline maps in this publication were obtained from http://www.d-maps.com/. Wine regions were added by authors and are approximate only.

Talking Points

- *Isn't it fascinating that the French are so committed to the concept of terroir (tear whar), defined below, that they don't even have a word for "winemaker"?*
- *Isn't it instructive that to produce great wines grapevines have to struggle for survival? They're sort of like people in that respect, don't you agree?*
- *It's so ironic that the great wines of Europe are made from grapes which get their nutrients through rootstocks from Texas!*

Six things to remember about wine:

1. **The world of wine is divided into *Old* and *New*. Old World wine is wine that is made in the European countries of France, Italy, Spain, Portugal, Germany, Austria and other countries of Europe. New World wine is made outside of Europe in the countries of South Africa, Australia, New Zealand, Canada, United States, Argentina, Chile and other countries outside of Europe.**
2. **Old World vineyards have cooler climates and thus produce more acidic wines. New World vineyards have warmer climates and thus produce more fruit-forward wines.**
3. **Old World wines are named for the region in which they are produced, such as Bordeaux or Chianti. The New World wines are named for the grapes from which they are made, such as Cabernet Sauvignon or Sangiovese.**

4. The Old World has strict laws regarding what grapes can be planted where. All red Burgundies must be made from Pinot Noir, or they cannot be called Burgundy. The New World has no such laws, and while some regions of the New World do quite well with a particular grape, such as Napa and Cabernet Sauvignon, the winemakers of the New World are free to grow any grapes they want and still put the name of the region on the bottle. In other words, the region of the New World will not tell you the grapes of the wine.

5. There are seven noble grapes. The four red noble grapes are Cabernet Sauvignon, Merlot, Pinot Noir and Syrah. The three white noble grapes are Chardonnay, Sauvignon Blanc and Riesling. What makes these grapes stand out above all others, and there are thousands of others, is that they have a good sugar/acid balance, they have a consistent flavor profile, they produce wines with enough structure that they can age well, and they can be grown successfully in many parts of the world.

6. When a wine is professionally evaluated, it is evaluated for both structure and aroma. The structure is made up of four elements: acidity, alcohol, tannins, if any, and residual sugar, if any. What is most important to the quality of the wine is that the elements are in balance with each other. We will discuss the typical aromas for each grape in chapter 16 of this book.

Grape Growing and Winemaking

While the details of grape growing and winemaking are rarely discussed in social settings, there are a few basics which may come up and which you need to know.

Vitis vinifera grapes rule. Wine can be made from anything that contains sugar, like apples and peaches. But all of the great wines of the world are made from grapes, specifically from those of the species *Vitis vinifera* (vee tis ven if a rhaa), commonly called the European wine grape. Native American species, most usually *Vitis labrusca* (la brews caa), are still made into wine on the east coast, but they produce pungent wines, often characterized as *foxy,* which are not to the liking of those used to the European style of wine.

Terroir. This is a word related to another French word for dirt. But it encompasses much more than just the soil on which grapes are grown. It also includes the climate, sun exposure, pests in the area, weather, proximity of water and topography. Obviously, some *terroirs* are better suited for some grape varieties than others, a matter explored earliest and most extensively by French *vignerones* (veen air own), which simply means "grape grower."

Some aspects of finding good *terriors* are counterintuitive. The best wines very much tend to come from nutrient-poor, well-drained soils in areas that experience dramatic daily temperature swings. The heat is believed to be a positive factor for the ripening/sugar development process. Cold nights are thought to help preserve the counterbalancing acidity without which a wine would be *flabby,* that is without the acidic structure needed to hold the wine together.

New Zealand represents an excellent example of the evolution of thinking about an industry's use of *terrior*. Initially, vineyards were planted on fertile plains on the warm North Island. As the New Zealand wine industry has evolved, however, grape vines are increasingly being planted on hillsides on the cooler South Island.

Phylloxera. The very name "*Phylloxera*" (phil ox errr ah) evokes in the minds of wine buffs the most disastrous, near-cataclysmic event in the history of wine. The dramatic occurrences described below were caused by a microscopic bug, a plant louse, technically an aphid. It is native to North America, and the foxy wine-producing grape vines of this continent have developed an immunity to its ravages. During the mid-Nineteenth Century, however, the pest was accidentally imported into Europe where it almost completely devastated the vineyards of that continent. A Texan, T. V. Morrison, came up with a solution to the crisis which was very much of the, "If you can't lick um, join um" type. He supplied the Europeans with native American rootstock onto which they grafted their *vinifera* grape vines. *Phylloxera* later invaded the vineyards of California, and they too had to be replanted on American rootstock. There are, however, places where *vinifera* grape vines are able to thrive on their own rootstock and do not have to be grafted.

The miracle of turning grape juice into wine. If grapes were merely left alone in some kind of natural bowl, like a depression in a rock, the skins over time would break down, exposing the juice to the air. In the air there are yeasts, microscopic entities which live along the borderline between plants and animals. These yeasts begin working on the sugars in the grape juice, converting them into carbon dioxide gas and alcohol. This is the process known as fermentation (firm men tay shun). When the alcohol level rises to between 12 and 15 percent, depending on the strain of yeast, the yeasts will be killed by their own product, the alcohol. All of the sugar may or may not have been converted in this fashion, depending largely on how much sugar was in the *must,* the liquid being turned into wine. If any remains, this is referred to as *residual sugar* and will give the wine a sweet taste, naturally. This sequence of events sets a limit to the potency of natural, that is unfortified, wines. Crude as it is, the resulting liquid in the depression in our rock can properly be referred to as "wine." Of course, winemakers, particularly in the New World, have learned ways to improve upon this naturally-occurring alcoholic beverage, and we'll discuss some of these methods in bringing this introductory chapter to a conclusion.

White versus Red. There are, of course, both red and white grapes. But with a few exceptions, the juice of both is clear. The color of red wine, therefore, comes from the skins. The longer the must is left on the skins, the darker red in color will be the resulting wine, ranging from a light rosé with little skin contact to a deep, dark red reflecting an extended period of time left on the skins. It is from the skins that tannin (tan in) comes, which gives red wines their leathery, mouth-drying quality.

"Maloing" a white wine. Malolactic (mal o lack tic) is the name of a possible second fermentation which greatly affects the characteristics of white wines such as Chardonnay (char doe nay). The winemaker can exercise control over this process which converts malic acid, such as is in apples, into lactic acid, as in milk. Obviously, a Chardonnay that has been "maloed" will be less crisp and acid-tasting and more round and buttery.

Another way to make a Chardonnay rounder and fuller is to leave it for a while on the "lees," the sediment that has settled out from the yeast and other particles. This process is called "sur lie aging" (sir lee). The lees may even be stirred periodically to further increase the creamy quality of a wine, a process called *batonnage* (bat un agze). Later the wine is siphoned off the lees, which is called *racking.*

<u>*Aged in oak*</u>. Most reds and some whites are aged in barrels, usually made of French or American oak. Such barrel aging allows the components of the wine, particularly the tannins, to marry and soften. The oak also imparts its own qualities, usually described on tasting with such terms as *vanilla, chocolate or smoky.* New barrels made of American oak have a particularly strong influence of this type. For whites, this process makes wines somewhat darker and with more "mouth fullness" (heavier texture). In contrast, an un-oaked Chardonnay is often referred to as a "Naked Chardonnay" and will be lighter and crisper. Oak aging will also give wines a longer time to develop and mature.

<u>*Usually ready to drink*</u>. Despite all the hype about vintage (year the wine was made) and barrel and bottle aging, the great, great majority of wines sold in this country are ready to drink at the time they are purchased. But to impress your important guests, a good general rule is to serve whites that are two to three years old and reds in the three to five year range. Exceptions to these general rules will be noted in later chapters, and they will require special research on the part of the buyer, as well as make your purse or wallet a lot lighter!

EUROPE
AKA The Old World

CHAPTER 2

FRANCE

France has a history of making true quality wines which goes back to the Roman occupation of Gaul before the time of Christ. In fact, it is generally acknowledged, albeit sometimes grudgingly, that France has the longest fine wine tradition in the world. We, in fact, believe that an understanding of French wines is in many ways a key to understanding all of the wines of the world, a point-of-view we will explain at the conclusion of this chapter.

Four things to remember about French wines:

1. **France is home to six of the seven noble grapes, Cabernet Sauvignon, Merlot, Pinot Noir, Syrah, Sauvignon Blanc and Chardonnay. The seventh noble grape, Riesling, originated in Germany.**
2. **Most other European countries have based their wine laws on the wine laws of France.**
3. **Many Old and New World countries base their wine-making techniques on those first used in France.**
4. **The main red grapes of Bordeaux are Cabernet Sauvignon and Merlot. The main red grape of Burgundy is Pinot Noir. Chablis, Champagne and white Burgundy are all made from Chardonnay.**

Bordeaux

Bordeaux is the most glamorized wine area of France, indeed of the world. As can be seen from the map, it sits on the southwest coast of France. The Gironde (zheer owned) River, which flows past the City of Bordeaux on its way north to the Atlantic Ocean, is the major landmark for identifying vineyards and wine styles in this region.

Bordeaux is home to numerous châteaux (shat toe) which really do resemble the magnificent wine estates which come to mind when one thinks about European wines. Many châteaux are, indeed, manicured vineyards and grounds and a winery surrounding a castle-like mansion. However, most wine-making operations outside of Bordeaux, and even many within it, are far less grand.

First Growths. In 1855, Emperor Napoleon III ordered a ranking of Bordeaux wines for use at an upcoming World's Fair. Going primarily on current prices, many of the châteaux of the Left or west bank of the Gironde were so ranked into First through Fifth Growths. The term *Growth,* as used here, refers to the producer and not to the specific characteristics of the grapes going into the wines, such as vine age. The four châteaux selling the most expensive wines were classified as *First Growths.* This number was much later increased to five châteaux, as discussed below. The point is that the term *First Growth* refers only to the very expensive wines made by just five Left Bank Bordeaux châteaux. The social implication here is that if you hear someone brag, "I only drink First Growth wines," you will realize how highly improbable such an assertion is and recognize that the speaker doesn't actually know as much about wines as he seems to be claiming. It would, of course, be the height of foolishness to confront a client with this wine-knowledge deficiency, but an understanding of an individual's apparent level of wine knowledge can be very important in successfully entertaining him or her, as also discussed below.

Left Bank versus Right Bank

The wines of the Left Bank and Right Bank differ because they feature different grapes in the *blends* they produce. That's right! Despite all the hype regarding California single varietal bottlings, the great and prestigious wines of Bordeaux are blends.

The Left Bank star grape is Cabernet Sauvignon (cab er nay saw veen yawn). Cabernet Sauvignon produces a very tannic, structured wine, often described as being *angular* in its early years in the bottle. As a result, the higher-priced Left Bank Bordeaux wines are often *cellared,* that is aged, for years to allow the tannins to soften and the angles to be incorporated into the body of the wine. These usually expensive bottles, thus, represent an exception to the general rule about wines being ready to drink at the time of purchase.

The star of the Right Bank is Merlot (mare low). It produces a soft, *jammy* wine which is more likely to be enjoyable early after bottling than its Left Bank cousins. Merlot, though, is used in the Left Bank to fill in the *mid-pallet*, or middle of the taste experience, with jammy fruit, thus softening the very structured primary grape.

The other three grapes in the Bordeaux blend may be Malbec (mall beck), Cabernet Franc (frank) and Petit Verdot (puh tea vare doe). Malbec, as we will see in the chapters on New World wines, went on to become a star in Argentina. Cabernet Franc is used in other parts of France, and a member of the prominent Mondavi (mon da vee) wine family believes this grape has quite a future in California. Petit Verdot, though, is more like the story of two brothers. One went to sea, and the other became Vice President. You know, neither was ever heard from again!

The Left Bank of Bordeaux illustrates nicely the type of quality ranking system used in France and, with variations, throughout Europe. It is called the AOC system, which stands for *Appellation d'Origine Controlée* (apple lass cee own door ee zheen control ay), which, basically, guarantees that a wine comes from that area of France and was made in conformity with the standards for that area. France, as a member of the European Union, is supposed to be moving toward the EU AOP system, which substitutes *Protégé* (pro tay zhay) for Controlée, but the French seem to be very much dragging their feet in making this conversion. Unlike in the New World, European wine ranking systems specify not only geographical areas but also allowed grape varieties, fermentation and viticultural techniques and aging requirements.

Talking Points

- *It's an interesting story how Baron Rothschild was able in 1973 to pull some political strings and get Mouton elevated from Second to First Growth. You know, that's the only change that has ever been made to the 1855 classification.*
- *You know, the British called Bordeaux reds "Clarets" from the French word for "red." I've heard that they used to be a lighter shade of red than they are today.*
- *Drinking a DRC(described below) is so on my bucket list!*
- *I'll drink some Beaujolais Nouveau again this year, you know, just to keep current my wine buff status!*
- *Did you know that there's as much pressure in a Champagne bottle as in the tires of an 18-wheeler?*
- *Funny how all the Champagne makers claim they use almost only Chardonnay and Pinot Noir. Wonder what happens to all the Pinot Meunier (moon yea) that's grown there?*
- *Pinot Meunier means "the miller's Pinot" because of the white flecks that appear on its leaves, which look like flour.*

- *The term sommelier (som el yea) comes from the French word "somme," which was the name of the cart that held the provisions for a noble family. Originally, the sommelier was in charge of the entire cart, both the food and the wine. Over time, however, the duties of a sommelier have been narrowed to the storage and service of wines, including guiding customers to wines they will appreciate.*
- *A friend of our family once really impressed everyone when he felt through a bag and announced that it contained "Rhine wine," obviously having felt the very long neck. I now realize that it might also have been a Mosel or an Alsatian wine, even a red. Wouldn't that be a kick to see a red wine pouring out of a Riesling-style bottle?*

All standard-meeting wines produced in Bordeaux qualify for the status of Appellation Bordeaux Contrôlée, which is usually spelled out toward the bottom of the front label. The Left Bank is also called the *Médoc* (may doc), and standard-meeting wines from this general area may be labeled properly Appellation Médoc Contrôlée. The southern part of this area, toward the City of Bordeaux, is called the Haut (oh) Médoc, and Appellation Haut Médoc Contrôlée wines are considered a cut above the rest. Within the Haut Médoc are located some of the most prestigious wine villages in the world. These include, moving north to south:

St-Estèphe (saunt-eh steff)
Pauillac (poo yak)
St-Julien (saun-zhewel ee awn)
Margaux (mar go)

Wines in which these village names are included between the A and the C of the AOC system are among the most exclusive and age-worthy wines in the world.

Most of us will never actually get to taste a First Growth, but yet and still we can all afford to talk about them! They may, thus, come up in your wine conversations, so here they are:

> Château Lafite-Rothschild (la feet-row shield), which is in Pauillac
>
> Château Latour (la tour), also in Pauillac
>
> Château Mouton-Rothschild (moo tawn). This is the new one, added in 1973.
>
> Château Margaux in Margaux
>
> Château Haut-Brion (oh-bree on), which is actually south of the Haut Médoc and in an area we'll discuss later

The Right Bank which, again, produces softer, Merlot-based blends, has classification systems in place, including the AOC system, but they are less discussed than are those on the opposite bank. And remember that the 1855 rankings and the quality term "Growth" are only applicable to Left Bank Bordeaux wines!

Two of the main quality wine-making communes of the Right Bank, going from northwest to southeast, are Pomerol (pom er all) and Saint-Emilion (saunt-uh meal ee on).

South of the City of Bordeaux

White wine production here is concentrated in the south, particularly in the areas of Graves (grahv), which is so-named for its gravel soil and is the location of First Growth Château Haut-Brion, and the regions Barsac (bar sack) and Sauternes (saw turn).

The whites of Bordeaux are made primarily from two varietals, Sauvignon Blanc (blonk) and Sémillon (say me yown). Sauvignon Blanc alone produces a light, crisp wine, and it has gone on to become a superstar in New Zealand. Sémillon, by contrast, is rounder and adds body to these white Bordeaux blends.

A famous, sweet dessert wine is a product of Sauternes and is known by that name. It is made when the grapes, primarily Sémillon, are attacked by a fungal disease called botrytis (bo try tis) during the humid falls of this coastal region. Botrytis, popularly called *noble rot,* draws water out of the grapes, producing a very high sugar content within the remaining liquid, leading to a luscious, honey-like wine. The most famous of these dessert wines is made by Château d'Yquem (dee kem).

Burgundy

The reds of Burgundy and Bordeaux are often discussed as being opposites. Whereas Bordeaux tend to be tannic and angular, the reds of Burgundy are softer and lighter in color. Some, in fact, have described Bordeaux as *masculine* and Burgundies as *feminine.* They have even, traditionally, been presented in differently shaped bottles. Note that the angular wine is in a high, sharp-shouldered bottle and the softer wine is in a soft, sloped-shouldered bottle.

The picture below depicts the three main bottle shapes. The bottle on the left is called a "long neck," and it is used for Rieslings. The bottle in the center is a Bordeaux bottle. The bottle on the right is a Burgundy bottle.

There is actually a functional reason for these different bottle shapes. As noted earlier, Bordeaux reds often require more aging to soften their tannins. During this aging process, sediment is likely to fall to the bottom of the bottle. This sediment may be trapped in the shoulder of a Bordeaux bottle to prevent it from going into your guests' glasses, a technique which is much less frequently needed in pouring Burgundy-style wines.

!WARNING! While we do try to prevent sediment from getting into glasses, this is only for aesthetic reasons. The sediment is completely harmless, being just solidified tannins. Should you pour out a glass of good wine because of such sediment, your act here will brand you as someone lacking in wine sophistication!

Burgundy is very easy to understand in one way – there is only one principal white wine grape and one main red.

The white is one we've met before – Chardonnay. And, as implied earlier, this is a very flexible wine grape in that its handling in the winery makes a tremendous difference in the qualities of the resulting wine. We will see some of the various styles of Chardonnay-based wines here in France.

The red wine grape of Burgundy is Pinot Noir (pee no new ahr), meaning the "black pinot." The "pinot" here means "pine" because of the pinecone-like shape of this grape's clusters. You will note as we go through the world of wine that many grapes have the word "pinot" in their names. This is because the Pinot family is very genetically unstable and has spawned many varietals, both red and white.

Pinot Noir itself is known as a very finicky grape in that it is difficult to cultivate, so much so that it has been nicknamed the *heartbreak grape.* So, fittingly, it produces a very delicate wine. Practically all European "Pinots" are delicate, but, as we shall see when we discuss New World wines, there are ways to make Pinot Noir into a more robust, darker wine.

The Geography of Burgundy

The first geographical factor of importance is that Burgundy is inland and northeast of Bordeaux. This inland location gives the area a continental climate, and continental climates involve at least some <u>cold</u>. We will see as we travel through the world of wine that quality Pinot Noirs and Chardonnays tend to be associated with cooler growing areas.

Immediately below are the communes/villages of Burgundy. This famous wine-producing area does, indeed, run north-south, but the sub-divisions aren't as neatly stacked one on top of the other as presented here. But this will give you a general idea of what's where in Burgundy.

Chablis (shah blee)

Côte d'Or (coat door)
Côte de Nuits (new e)

Marsannay (mar san ay)
Fixin (feex un)
Gevrey-Chambertin (zhev ray-sham
bear teen)
Morey-St-Denis (mo ray-saun-den knee)
Chambolle-Musigney (shom bowl-moo
sih nyee)
Vougeot (voo zhee oh)
Flagey-Échezeaux (flah jhay-ay she zo)
Vosne-Romanée (vos nay-rome ah nay)
Nuits-St-Georges (new ee-saun zhorzhe)
Côte de Beaune (coat de bone)
Aloxe-Corton (al ahs-core ton)
Beaune
Pommard (po mar)
Volnay (vohl nay)
Meursault (mare so)
Puligny-Montrachet (poo lean yee-mon
rah shay)
Chassagne-Montrachet (sha saun-mon
rah shay)

Côte Chalonnaise (shall o nace)

Mâconnais (mah con nay)

While both whites and red wines are produced throughout Burgundy, a wine called merely Burgundy, or in French Bourgogne (burr go n'yeh), will be assumed to be red, as opposed to a white Burgundy. White wine output tends to be concentrated in the northern and southern parts of this region, particularly in Chablis and Mâcon. The wines of Chablis are crisp and flinty, partly because of the soil, which contains a lot of limestone, a continuation of the dramatic White Cliffs of Dover in England. Chardonnays made further south are rounder and fuller than the wines of Chablis.

The Côte d'Or means coast of gold in French. The reference here is to the golden color that the vineyards turn in the fall and not to prospecting for gold. The most prestigious red wines are from the Cote de Nuits north of the City of Beaune. Here is located the famed Domaine de la Romanée Conti (dough men de la roman nay con tea). So impressed was the City of Vosne with this fabulous property within its boundary that it appended the name Romanée to the village's official name, as shown above. This is a common practice in Burgundy, so don't make the mistake of assuming that the name of a famous vineyard on the label means that the wine actually came from that parcel of land. Only when the vineyard name alone is on the label would such a conclusion be justified. Another clue to authenticity is that you will have to shell out big bucks for these exclusive wines!

A wine from Domaine de la Romanée Conti is familiarly called a *DRC*, even by wine buffs who, like your authors, have never even been in the same building with one of these rare and breathtakingly expensive wines. DRC, like most upscale Burgundian vineyards, is small, owing to the inheritance laws which have been in place in this part of France. Limited supply, obviously, contributes to higher prices.

In addition to the AOC system, there is also a regional quality rating system in place here in Burgundy. Some vineyards are allowed to use the designation *Premier Cru* or *Gran Cru*, with this term Cru (crew) being roughly equivalent to the Bordeaux classifications of Growths.

But, unlike in Bordeaux, Grand Cru is a higher rating than Premier (First) Cru. Another difference between the two regions relates to the fact that whereas when a Bordeaux château acquires more land, its rating extends to the new property, this is not so in Burgundy. Here the status attaches to particular and carefully defined and designated parcels of land, specifically and only, forever and forever, amen!

Beaujolais

South of Burgundy sits a quite distinct wine area called Beaujolais (bo ju lay). This upbeat, kind of frivolous name does, indeed, give you a hint as to the characteristics of the wines made here. The words *light* and *fruity* come to mind when one thinks of Beaujolais. This is a picnic wine, good for both sipping outdoors and drinking with simple informal dishes, such as the quintessentially American hot dog, as well as deviled eggs and roast chicken. Despite being a red wine, knowledgeable wine drinkers will often serve it slightly chilled.

The wine grape employed here is the Gamay (gaah may), a grape which, obviously, tends to produce fruity wines. This fruitiness is enhanced by a special wine-making technique which is used almost exclusively here. It's called *carbonic maceration* or *whole berry fermentation*. Essentially, grapes are covered by carbon dioxide (CO_2). In this oxygen-free environment, the grapes break down internally, producing alcohol without the intervention of yeasts, instead relying on natural enzymes within the grapes. This sequence of events results in a wine which is low in tannins, high in tropical fruit aromas and ready to drink very soon after bottling. Obviously, most Beaujolais do not require aging.

The AOC system is also in place here in Beaujolais, with, as throughout most of France, smaller areas being more prestigious than larger areas. There are "in" villages, but since this is a more frivolous wine, these specific AOCs are not discussed as often as is the case in Bordeaux and Burgundy. That having been said, however, it may prove important to know that there are 38 villages with elevated status, and these Appellation Beaujolais-Villages Contrôlée wines are considered superior to simple Appellation Beaujolais Contrôlée wines. There are also 10 Cru Beaujolais which are both good and readily available. In this category, you will frequently see wines from the communes of Morgan (more gone) and Fleurie (flur ee) in local stores.

Beaujolais creates one of the great rituals of the wine year. After harvest each fall, some of the grapes are quickly turned into wine and trucked to Paris where these wines are released for consumption at the stroke of midnight on the third Thursday in November, thus helping to kick off the Holiday Season. Others around the world are able to participate in this annual celebration as well, and wine producers in this region ship bottles of this *Beaujolais Nouveau* (new vo, which does, indeed mean new) across the globe in preparation for this date. An alert distributor/wine bar owner should, thus, offer her patrons this wine at 3:00 PM on the west coast of the U.S. on the Wednesday before the third Thursday in November, which would be midnight in Paris!

Despite all the hype, Beaujolais Nouveau is a simple, fruity wine. But, every year, its release creates a fun tradition!

The Rhône Valley

The Rhône Valley is the area along the Rhône River, which rises in Switzerland and flows south through southeast France until emptying into the Mediterranean Sea west of Marseille. This area is best known for its red wines, but it is a red wine area with a dual personality, with the northern and southern parts being very different in terms of grapes used and wines made.

The primary grape of the Northern Rhône is Syrah (sir ahh), which produces a very fruity, spicy and tannic wine. It is sometimes used as a stand-alone varietal, as in Cornas (corn oz). These Syrah-based wines are so full and robust that in years past they were snuck into Bordeaux and Burgundy to bolster the substance of their wines. In other parts of the Northern Rhône, such as in Côte Rôtie (row t) and Hermitage (air me tahzhe), this large red grape is blended with white grapes, Viognier (vee un yay) in Côte Rôtie and Roussanne (rue saun) and Marsanne (mar saun) in Hermitage, to add a more delicate and perhaps floral taste to the resulting wines.

The Southern Rhône produces much more wine than the Northern Rhône (96% v. 4%), and the great bulk of the southern wines are red (84%). The red wines of the Southern Rhône are blends of 18 authorized grape varieties. The leading grape here is Grenache (gren ahsh). This is one of the few grapes used by the French which is not indigenous to France. It is actually native to Spain, where it is called Garnacha (gar nah cha). Grenache produces a wine which is high in alcohol, causing a *hot* feel in your mouth. This *heat* is moderated by blending in other grape varieties. The most frequent blending partners here are Syrah and Mourvedre (moo ved rah). Putting together the first letters of the names of these grapes results in the acronym *GSM*. GSM, thus, refers to this Southern Rhône blend, whether made in the Southern Rhône or not.

Some of the important areas of the Southern Rhône which may come up in wine conversations are Châteauneuf-du-Pape (shaw toe nuf-du-pop), Gigondas (zhee gon das) and Vacqueyras (vac a rah).

Châteauneuf-du-Pape literally means "the new home of the pope" and got that name because it is close to Avignon where the popes resided for most of the Fourteenth Century. In honor of that association, many wines from this area have a version of the Papal Seal, featuring the Keys of Saint Peter, embossed on these Burgundy-shaped bottles. Another interesting feature of this area is that glaciers left rocks, called here *galets* (gah lay), in what became the vineyards of the Southern Rhône. These rocks retain the heat from the sun, hastening ripening and contributing to these being big, boozy, flavorful wines.

Another important area of the Southern Rhone is Tavel (tuh vel), which makes a Grenache-based rosé of the same name. To the east of here, extending to the Italian border, lies the sun-drenched area of Provence (pro vohnce). While a perfect place for artists to work, it is best known in the wine world for its AOC rosés, which are made from the same grapes used in the Southern Rhône.

Rosés have taken a PR beating on the cocktail circuit because of the slightly sweet and effervescent Portuguese rosés and the lamentable California White Zinfandel. But rosés can actually be quite pleasant and subtly fruity. As we'll see, they may be a wonderful pairing for informal, slightly spicy dishes, like cloved ham and lavender-rubbed salmon. In fact, no less than Star Couple Angelina Jolie and Brad Pitt are making a rosé called Miraval on their

Provence vineyard site. So, don't be surprised if rosé becomes the Cinderella wine of the next few years.

Speaking of Cinderella wines….

Champagne

Now we reverse our northerly course through France and visit the extreme northeastern area of Champagne.

Champagne is certainly the most romantic name in wine. It conjures up images of celebrations and elegant parties attended by glamorous young women, perhaps even wearing glass slippers! But this fashionable sparkling wine was actually born of frustration and despair.

The Champenoise (sham pen wahz) wanted to make fine wines, like all true French men and women. So they would pick their grapes, crush them and, when the fermentation process appeared to have stopped, bottle the resulting wine.

But in the spring, the wines in the bottles would start to bubble, and many would actually explode. The wine was, thus, considered regrettably flawed. What the winemakers didn't realize was that the fermentation last fall wasn't stopped because the yeast had been killed by the rising alcohol level. No, the cold had merely rendered them dormant. And when it warmed up in Champagne in the spring, they became active again and resumed their mission of turning sugar into alcohol and carbon dioxide. But the gas, having nowhere to go, was trapped in the bottle, building up ever-increasing pressure and leading to dangerous explosions.

Eventually, they learned to control this process by putting their wine in extra-thick bottles. Also, they learned to pick and ferment early and then introduce a sugar solution into the wine, which causes a second fermentation in that bottle, which is responsible for the bubbles in modern Champagne. This sugar solution is called the Liqueur de Tirage (liquer de tier agze).

The sediment from the second fermentation is removed through an elaborate set of procedures. Firstly, the bottles are placed in a stand in which their necks point downward. As time goes forward, they are twisted slightly and repeatedly, a process called "riddling" (pronounced just as it looks). As soon as the floating materials have been thus helped to move to the neck of the bottles, the necks are quickly frozen, as in a mixture of water, salt and ice. The temporary cap is then removed, and the pressure in the bottle forces the resulting ice plug out through the opening. This procedure is called the dégorgement (day gorzhe mahn).

The wine that was thus lost is replaced along with varying amounts of cane sugar. It is the amount of sugar in this "dosage" (doe sazhe) that determines the final level of sweetness of a Champagne. In order from driest to sweetest, these levels are:

Brut Nature.........Bone dry
Extra Brut..........Very dry
Brut..................Dry
Extra Dry...........Off dry
Sec..................Semi-sweet
Demi-Sec...............Sweet
Doux (DO).........Very sweet

The grapes used to make Champagne are Chardonnay, Pinot Noir and Pinot Meunier. By removing the skins quickly from the black grapes a *Blanc de Noirs* (white from black) wine is produced. A Champagne made entirely from Chardonnay is, accordingly, called a *Blanc de Blancs.*

Because the grapes are harvested early to produce high acid/low sugar wines for blending into the base pre-Liqueur de Tirage wine, Champagne has a lean, crisp taste. Its smell is toasty.

All but the most exceptional Champagnes are blends of wines initially fermented in different years. They may, thus, be labeled NV, which in this case stands for *non-vintage,* not Nevada.

The term Champagne is only properly applied to sparkling wines made here. Such wines made elsewhere may include the description Méthode Traditionelle (may toad tra deece cee o nel) but never Methode Champenoise, which is also restricted to use here. Even other French producers of traditionally-made sparkling wines must call them a Cremant (cray mawn).

Champagne, like other wines, is usually bought and sold in the 750 milliliter bottle, although it will appear larger because of the increased thickness of the glass. Smaller sizes, the Split (187 ml) and the Demi (375 ml), are good for individual consumption and for couples. There are dramatically larger sizes as well, which are named after Old Testament characters like Methuselah (8 bottles) and Nebuchadnezzar (20 bottles). While these huge bottles make wonderful displays in restaurants, they are actually only rarely served, and even most sommeliers have forgotten how much wine each of them holds.

The Loire Valley

The Loire (lou are) is France's longest river. It runs from south-central France up toward Paris and then west until it flows into the Atlantic. Its banks contain big agricultural sections which are often referred to collectively as the Garden of France. This wine-producing area is not as frequently discussed as are others in France, but there are several things you should know about the Loire.

The Loire Valley is best known for its white wines. The central part of the valley, south of Paris, is home to our old Bordeaux friend Sauvignon Blanc. An important sub-region to know here is Pouilly Fumé (pooey fu may). This area is not to be confused with the sound-alike Pouilly Fuissé (fu say), which is in the before-reviewed Mâconnais of Burgundy and, of course, makes wines from Chardonnay. Going back to the Loire, though, fumé means smoke in French. Traditionally, this smoky taste represented a crisp reflection of the limestone and flint in the soils of that general area. Later, some producers here began to oak their Sauvignon Blancs to add more smoke to the taste, a practice which is not typical of Pouilly Fumés. And when we study the wines of California, we'll see that the word Fumé was appropriated there as a marketing strategy to describe an oaked and, thus, somewhat smoky Sauvignon Blanc.

About half-way between Pouilly Fumé and the Atlantic lies the important commune of Vouvray (vouv ray). Wines from here are made from 100% of the white grape Chenin Blanc (shen in). This grape produces wines that are quite variable in style, but at their best they can be full and fruity, ideal for sipping but with enough acidity to make them food-friendly.

Chenin Blanc isn't seen that often as a stand-alone varietal, except in South Africa where it's called *Steen* (pronounced as it looks). This grape is, though, extensively used in California's Central Valley to produce jug wines.

Red wines along the Loire are made primarily from Cabernet Franc, which we met earlier as a Bordeaux blending grape. An important area of production here is Chinon (she non).

Traveling south from the Loire, back toward the Mediterranean, we go through or near some alcoholic beverage-producing areas deserving of mention.

Madiran (ma dee rahn) here in southwest France makes a rustic and tannic red wine from Tennat (ten aht). Further north, Tennat may be blended with Malbec, the primary grape in the "Black Wine of Cahors (ka hors)."

North of Bordeaux on the Atlantic coast is Cognac (con yak). Also along this coast but south of Bordeaux lies Armagnac (arm men yahk). These two areas produce brandies, which are hard liquors made by distilling wine principally from the Ugni Blanc (ug knee blahnk) grape. Scotch and Irish and American whiskeys, by contrast, are essentially distilled beers.

Just as we approach the Mediterranean coast we're in Languedoc-Roussillon (lawn gwi doc rue cee yon). This has always been a bulk wine production area for the thirsty French, but quality wines are increasingly being made here. These higher-quality wines often include Merlot and Cabernet Sauvignon, as well as rosés. The country wines from this region are often labeled Pays d'Oc (pay ee doc).

Alsace

Alsace (all sauce) is the great exception to all we've learned about French wines. Positioned along the German border, its wine industry tends to have more in common with German than French wine-makers. This is the only area of France in which wines are labeled according to the kind of grape. The two main grapes used here are Gewurztraminer (ga vertz tra meaner - *gerwz* means "spicy" in German) and Riesling (re sling), which is actually the signature grape of Germany. Alsatian wines that are readily available here tend to have some residual sugar, so they are pleasant for just sipping and enjoying with spicy Asian dishes.

The Key to the Wines of France
Or
Is France the Key to the Wines of the World?
(The answer is YES!)

Below is presented a "schematic" of the wine-producing areas of France:

<u>Champagne</u>
Chardonnay
Pinot Noir
Pinot Meunier

<u>Loire</u>
Sauvignon Blanc
Chenin Blanc
Cabernet Franc

<u>Alsace</u>
Riesling
Gewurztraminer
Pinot Gris

<u>Burgundy</u>
Chardonnay
Pinot Noir

<u>Bordeaux</u>
Cabernet Sauvignon
Merlot
Malbec
Cabernet Franc
Sauvignon Blanc

<u>Beaujolais</u>
Gamay

<u>Rhone</u>
Syrah
Viognier
Grenache

<u>Southwestern France</u>
Tennat
Cabernet Savignon
Merlot

Please look at this chart, particularly the names of the italicized grapes. Where have you seen/heard these names before? That's right! These are the names of the wines you're served at every art exhibit, on by-the-glass wines lists in local restaurants, etc. Now you know "the rest of the story"/from whence they came!

Looking forward to our exploration of the "New World," a story that is so often repeated is of people wanting to make fine wines realizing that their area has commonalities with a certain area of France. They reason that, perhaps, the grapes that do well in that part of France will make good wines here as well. And they're usually right!

As we'll see when we study California, the big exception to "The French Connection" is Zinfandel.

CHAPTER 3

ITALY

Four things to remember about Italian wine are:

1. Chianti (kee ahn tee) is from Tuscany.
2. Barolo (bah row lo) and Barbaresco (bar bah ress coe) are from Piedmont. These are the most important red wines of Italy. They each have a distinctive, balanced acidity.
3. Red wines from Italy are more acidic than red wines from other countries.
4. Italy grows over 2000 varieties of wine grapes, most of them are indigenous.

Only the size of Arizona, Italy is the largest producer and exporter of wine in the world. The country is quite diverse, with German being spoken in the northern part of the country, Trentino-Alto-Adige. From the southern island of Sicily one can see Africa with the naked eye. This geographic and cultural diversity is reflected in the wide range of Italian wines produced. In terms of global influence, however, Italy is behind France, not having the same long history of devotion to producing fine wines. Also, Italian grape varieties do not travel as well as their French counterparts. Whereas France is a country of noble, international grapes that are grown world-wide, Italy is a country of indigenous grapes that only do well in their homeland. However, Italy's status of number two is not like the runner-up in a beauty contest. Italy is, by-in-large, its own contest and a wine world apart.

When you look at a map of the wine regions of Italy, you will notice something interesting. Unlike every other country of Europe and the New World, the wine regions of Italy are not represented by isolated pockets. The entire country is a wine region. What is it about Italy that makes it so prolific with the grape? There are three things this country has going for it that make it close to perfect for wine-grape growing. First, the entire country is in an ideal latitude. All good vineyards are between the latitudes of 32 and 52 degrees north and south. Most of Italy is smack in the middle of that, between 40 and 45 degrees. Second, Italy is surrounded on three sides by water. Most vineyards are within 75 miles of a sea. Third, Italy is very hilly, putting most vineyards at higher altitudes. These three factors together, the latitude, the altitude and the proximity to water, all work to create a very moderate climate in the vineyards of Italy. A moderate climate means the grapes will develop a good balance between sugars and acids. Warm weather produces grapes with a high sugar content, which translates into a high alcohol wine. Cool weather produces grapes with a high acid content. Italy's moderate climate is just right, producing grapes with a good balance of sugar and acid. Italy's grapes are turned into wines that have medium alcohol content and good acidity. It's the acidity that makes Italian wines so food-friendly.

Tuscany: There are Tuscans...

Tuscany lies on the central western coast of Italy. Like much of Italy, it is a hilly region situated in the perfect latitude for grape growing. The higher altitudes of the hills create cooler temperatures for the Italian vineyards. Those cooler temperatures produce a more acidic grape. Acidity is the most food-friendly of all the wine elements. Why? It's because the acids in the wine cause the wine consumer to salivate. Within the saliva are enzymes that break down the food and release its aromas and flavors. When you drink an acidic wine with a meal, you experience the flavors of the meal more fully. This is good to know when you are ordering wine in a restaurant. We are not suggesting that you have Italian wine with every meal, but, if you want a red wine with good acidity, look to Italy. It is the hills of Italy that create the food-friendly, acidic red wines we have grown to love.

Chianti is made from the Sangiovese (sahn joe vay zay) grape. It is an acidic red wine with medium body, medium tannins and lots of red fruit aromas. If you taste tangy sour cherries, you are tasting Chianti. Some people find the acidity of Chianti off-putting. But, again, it is the acidity that makes Chianti so food-friendly. Alone, it is a bit tart, but with a piece of Italian sausage or salami, or even a simple pasta dish with tomatoes, the wine comes alive. Chianti is a wine you will want to experience with food, especially Italian food.

Tuscany is one of 20 administrative regions in Italy. Chianti is a major wine region within Tuscany. And within the Chianti DOCG (Denominazione Di Orignine Controllata E Garantita or high quality level wine) are seven sub-regions where Chianti is made. The most common sub-region is Rufina. Chianti Classico is a DOCG unto itself. Wines from these two regions, Rufina and Chianti Classico, are readily available in stores and often listed on restaurant menus here in the US. All wines with the Chianti Rufina and Chianti Classico DOCG are made primarily from the Sangiovese grape.

Another common Chianti you may find in stores is packaged in a straw basket. That basket is called a "fiasco," and it certainly was for the reputation of Chianti in American markets. Popular in the US in the 1950's through the 1970's, the straw fiasco came to be associated with simple, rustic wines. As the quality of Italy's exports to the US have improved, however, wine makers have wanted to disassociate themselves from the straw basket of times gone by. Nowadays, most quality Chiantis are sold in the Bordeaux style, square-shouldered bottle.

Tuscany: ...And There are Super-Tuscans

Along the coast of Tuscany is a region called Maremma (ma reh ma), the birthplace of Super Tuscans. The winemakers of Tuscany, as in most Old World wine regions, must adhere to strict laws when it comes to grape growing and wine making. There are laws dictating the yields of the grape vines, the regions where the grapes can be grown, the alcohol level of the wine, the length of time the wine ages and the type of grapes used to make the wine. While Chianti blends may contain some international variety grapes, the law states that in basic Chianti at least 70% of the blend must be Sangiovese. In Chianti Classico, it is 80%. Most of the other grapes used in the blend are indigenous, that is native to Italy. In the 1970's, winemakers in the Maremma region of Tuscany wanted to use less Sangiovese and blend it with more international varieties, that is varieties that can be grown in many parts of the world, such as Cabernet Sauvignon and Merlot. In doing so, they lost the privilege of using the Chianti or Chianti Classico DOCG name and rating on their wines. Super Tuscans are ranked as IGT (Indicazione Geografica Tipica) wines, a step below the DOC or DOCG ratings. But they are more often than not just as high quality as the traditional Chiantis. The French grapes blended into the Sangiovese create a more lush and textured wine with added dimensions of dark fruit aromas and bigger tannins. If you want to enjoy a good Italian wine but feel that Chianti is too acidic, try a Super-Tuscan. They have all the lushness of a Cabernet Sauvignon, while still maintaining that great Italian acidity. The wine bottles will not say "Super-Tuscan." However, many Tuscan (Toscana in Italian) wines with IGT on the label are Super-Tuscan blends. This is especially true if they are from a major producer such as Villa Antinori.

Eighty five percent of the wines made in Tuscany are red. Some other red grapes grown for wine in Tuscany are Brunello (brew nell oh,) Morellino (more reh lee no) and Prugnolo Gentile (prun yo lo gen teal ay). Not only are they all red grapes, they are all clones of the grape Sangiovese. That is to say, if you are drinking a red wine from Tuscany, whether it is a wine from the regions of Montalcino, Scansano, Montepulciano or Chianti, you are probably drinking Sangiovese.

If you are not drinking a Sangiovese wine in Tuscany, you might be drinking the region's specialty dessert wine, Vinsanto (veen sant oh.) This is not a wine to know about because it is common. It is a wine to know something about because it is fascinating. They are traditionally made from, what else but Sangiovese, or the white version made from Trebbiano (treb ee ah no - remember Ugni Blanc, the bland blender grape from France?) and Malvasia (mall vah zee ah). The grapes are harvested and then either hung out to dry or laid out on mats. This drying process, called appassimento (ah pah cee ment oh), concentrates the sugars in the grapes as their water content evaporates. Once dry, they are crushed and put into small barrels with the lees (dead yeast cells) of a previous vintage. That is to say, the barrels were not cleaned out before their second use. Using the lees from a previous vintage is believed to jump-start the fermentation process. The barrels are sealed tight and left to ferment and age for two to six years! Yes, we know, this sounds like a science experiment waiting to happen. And it may have begun as a mistake that turned out well. The wine is often sweet, but not always. It is, however, always full-bodied with nutty, "raisiny" aromas.

The Piedmont: Tar and Roses

Barolo and Barbaresco are two regions in the State of Piedmont. They are considered the most powerful wines in the world. They are both made from the Nebbiolo (neb ee oh lo) grape. They are full-bodied, dark and tannic but with good acidity and aromas of dark fruit and anise, often referred to as the wine of "tar and roses." A bit on the pricey side, in the stores they begin at around $40. Off a restaurant menu, the cost will be much greater. But what impressive wines they are! Barolo and Barbaresco are intense and complex wines that are an experience all to themselves but also go beautifully with big, heavy, flavorful meals, especially fatty red meats and rich earthy foods like Osso Buca and mushroom risotto.

If you like Cabernet Sauvignon and Syrah, you will love the Nebbiolo grape. Like a Cab or Syrah, Nebbiolo is dark, tannic and full-bodied. In Barolo and Barbaresco, the wine is unblended, 100% Nebbiolo. Adhering to strict laws, the wine is well aged and spends a good amount of time in oak, giving it traditional oak flavors such as wood, vanilla and chocolate.

Though Barolo and Barbaresco wines are not as common in stores and restaurants, they are certainly worth seeking out. They are big, powerful and very impressive. If you are dining with someone who enjoys Cabernet Sauvignon and you have the opportunity to introduce him or her to the Nebbiolo grape, you will want to take that opportunity. The Nebbiolo grape makes a lasting impression, and so will you.

Both Sangiovese and Nebbiolo are considered indigenous grapes. What does this mean? They have, for all practical purposes, only been grown successfully in their native regions of Tuscany and Piedmont, respectively. There are some exceptions, such as in Lombardy, Italy and the foothills of the Sierra in California. But the exceptions are few and far between. In general, if you want good Sangiovese and Nebbiolo, you'll need to get it from Tuscany and Piedmont.

Talking Points

- *Did you know that Italy grows over 2000 indigenous grapes that are used to make wine? Did you know that because of their great acidity, Italy's red wines are some of the most food-friendly reds on the planet?*
- *Super-Tuscans may be rated at a lower quality level than traditional Chianti, but they are full-bodied wines with layers of aromas and flavors.*
- *Italy is Goldilocks when it comes to vineyards. Its latitude, altitude and proximity to water make it just right for grape growing.*
- *A good Vinsanto can be left to ferment for up to six years!*
- *Appassimento is the process of drying grapes in order to intensify the sugar concentration. Passito describes the wines made by this process. So, a vinsanto is a passito wine made using the appassimento process.*

The Piedmont: Three Other Wines

In Northwestern Italy, in the Piedmont, there is grown a grape called Barbera (bar bare ah). Two primary regions for this grape within Piedmont are Alba and Asti. You will find the grape name and region right on the label of the wine bottle, as Barbera d'Alba and Barbera d'Asti. Barbera, like other Italian reds, is a medium alcohol and high acid wine. It has aromas of black cherries, plums and spice. Not as big a wine as Barolo or Barbaresco, Barbera is a medium-bodied wine that is food-friendly and quite satisfying.

Two thirds of the wine made in Piedmont is red. However, there is a well-known white wine that comes from Piedmont from the region of Asti. It is made from the Moscato (mo scot oh) grape. As is often the case, the wines of Italy are named as "grape of region." So it is with this highest volume wine of Piedmont. Moscato d'Asti is made using a process called "partial fermentation," meaning the fermentation is stopped before it is complete. Interrupting fermentation creates a wine that is sweet because of the residual sugar that was not fermented into alcohol, creating a wine that is low in alcohol. Partial fermentation creates a lightly sparkling wine that is referred to as "frizzanté." Moscato d'Asti's sister wine is Asti Spumonte. They differ in that Asti Spumonte is slightly higher in alcohol and more fully sparkling. Both sweet sparkling wines are made with the Moscato grape and have flavors of peach and apricot.

While there are many more wines made in Piedmont, there is one more wine with which you are already familiar. Vermouth, often used in Martinis and as a cooking wine with shellfish, is a fortified wine. That means that during or after fermentation, brandy or a grape-based alcohol is added to the wine. Obviously, the result is a very stable, very high alcohol wine. The Vermouth of Piedmont differs from Vermouth that you have seen in your local stores in the U.S. While our Vermouth is white and dry, the Vermouth of Piedmont is red and sweet.

The Veneto: Amorone, Prosecco and Trebbiano

In the northeastern side of Italy is a region called The Veneto (ven net oh). The wine you are most likely to hear about from this region is Amorone (aw ma row nay). Amorone is a blend of three indigenous red grapes, Corvina (core vee nuh), Molinara (mow lean ah rah) and Rondinella (ron dee nell uh). What is interesting about the wine is how it is made. Using the appasimento method, as was discussed earlier, the wine is fermented dry, that is there is no residual sugar, so, while Amorone is quite heavy-bodied and with high alcohol content, it is not at all unctuous. The result is a rich, "raisiny" flavored wine that is not sweet. Amorone is a lovely wine to enjoy after dinner with a plate of cheese and nuts.

Another well-known wine from The Veneto is made from the Glera (glare ah) grape. While you may not recognize it by that name, Glera is more commonly known as Prosecco (pro sec oh), a very popular sparkling wine. Made using the tank method rather than the traditional method of true Champagne, Prosecco is a light, fun bubbly wine that is readily available in stores at very affordable prices.

Before we leave The Veneto, there is another wine that you have probably seen in stores, if not tasted already. Does the name "Soave" (swa vay) sound familiar? It is a region in Veneto that is known for its white wine blend by the same name. The blend is of the indigenous grapes Garganega (gar guh neg ah) and Trebbiano and sometimes the international grape Chardonnay. It can be a light to medium-bodied, dry white wine with fruity aromas and some notes of almond. Interestingly, Trebbiano is Italy's most widely grown white grape, and because of its neutral flavors is used primarily as a blending grape. Though widely grown all over Italy, you will rarely see it as a single varietal. It is a silent partner in many blends.

Trentino-Alto-Adige: Who Am I to Dis a Gris?

The northern-most wine region of Italy is Trentino-Alto Adige (tren tee no-ahl toe ah dee zhay). Because of its proximity to Austria, much of the culture of the region, including the wine culture, has been shaped by the Germanic influence of this neighboring country. The wines are often labeled *varietally.* Varietal labeling is common in the New World and in Germany, but not in the rest of Europe, except in the region of Alsace in France. That is to say that rather than the wines being named for the region as is done in most of Europe, the wines are named for the grape as is done in Germany and the New World. There are also German wine varieties grown in this part of Italy, including Müller-Thurgau (moo ler-tur gow) and Traminer (tra mean er). Northern Italy has a cooler climate and does well growing the more acidic white grapes, although red grapes are grown here, too. The most prevalent grape grown here that you are most likely familiar with is Pinot Grigio (gree zhee oh). This grape in Alsace, France is known as Pinot Gris. It is the same grape. But the different names indicate a difference in style. To understand the difference, we have to talk a little about climate.

Alsace, France enjoys what is known as *the rain shadow effect.* What this means is that the clouds get hung up on the mountains, so the region east of the mountains gets a great deal of sunshine. The rain shadow effect is also a factor in Washington State, Argentina and the South Island of New Zealand. Because of the great amount of sunshine, grape growers in these regions are able to leave the grapes on the vines for a longer period of time. The longer the grapes are on the vines before harvest, the greater the sugar content of the grape. This will not necessarily produce a sweet wine. If allowed to ferment completely, it will produce a higher alcohol or more full-bodied wine. And that is the difference between Pinot Gris and Pinot Grigio. Pinot Gris is more full-bodied and rich. Pinot Grigio is more light and minerally. The flavors of the wine in either style are apple and pear with some honey and spice.

You will find the Pinot Grigio style from Italy, California and Australia. The Pinot Gris style comes from Alsace, France and Oregon.

Talking Point

- *Pinot Gris is a mutant of Pinot Noir, the genetically unstable red grape of Burgundy, France. They are also both related to Pinot Blanc.*

Some Minor Regions with Some Major Values

If you enjoy the acidic red wines of Italy but want to try less well-known but still readily available grapes, here are some suggestions. Many of these wines are from points south in Italy. And remember, as we move south we move toward warmer temperatures which produce less acidic grapes. However, even in the south Italian red wines are still acidic enough to be food-friendly.

In the region of Aburzzo (ah brewt zo) on the eastern central coast is a grape called Montepulciano (mont ah pull chee ah no). Following the "grape of region" formula, the name on the wine bottle will read, "Montepulciano d'Abruzzo." This is a very interesting wine that has flavors of dark berries, black olives and some spice. The structure of the wine is rustic. That is, it is not a smooth elegant wine but a casual, straight-forward wine that goes really well with pizza.

Talking Point

- *Montepulciano in Abruzzo is a grape. But in Tuscany there is a region called Montepulciano. The two, though sharing a name, have nothing to do with each other. The grape used to make wine in the region Montepulciano is Prugnolo Gentile which is, of course, a clone of Sangiovese. If you want a good pizza wine order the grape Montepulciano d'Abruzzo. If you want a good lasagna wine order the regional Vino Nobile de Montepulciano.*

Although red wines are more prevalent in Italy, the region that produces the greatest proportion of white wines is Latium, the home of Rome. Two wines from this region that you may be able to find in stores are Frascoti (fra scot ee) and Est! Est!! Est!!! di Montefiascone (mont tee fe ask oh nay). We didn't mean to be overly enthusiastic about the latter wine. The repetition and exclamation marks are part of the name of the wine. Both of these Latium white wines are made from a blend of two indigenous grapes, Trebbiano (remember our friend aka Ugni Blanc, the bland but abundant grape of Italy and France?) and Malvasia (mal vah zee ah.) You will learn more about Malvasia in Portugal where it is grown on the island of Madeira to produce a fortified wine of the same name. While Trebbiano is neutral, the flavors of Malvasia are fruity, such as peaches, apricots and raisins.

If you travel all the way to the boot of Italy to the region Apulia (ah pool e ah), you will find some familiar reds, including Sangiovese, our friend with many names in Tuscany, Barbera, the acidic red from Piedmont, Montepulciano, the grape from Abruzzo and Primitivo (pree me tee voh.) This latter has identical DNA to the grape we know in the U.S. as Zinfandel.

Talking Point

- *Primitivo/Zinfandel did not originate in Italy nor in California. The grape is originally from Croatia where it goes by the name Crljenak Kastelanski (tril yeh nak kah steh lan ski).*

There are three wines worth mentioning from the Island of Italy. Sicily produces a wine from the grape Nero d'Avola (nare oh da vo la). The wine has red fruit aromas with a rustic minerality. Sicily is also home to a wine you probably last had at a wedding dinner in a sauce served over chicken. Marsala is made from three white indigenous grapes, Catarratto (cot ah rot oh), Grillo (gree lo) and Inzolia (in zoh lee ah).

Sardinia's most famous grape is Cannonau (cah no naw). You're probably thinking it couldn't be that famous because you've never heard of it. In France it is known as Grenache. In Spain it is known as Garnacha (gar na cha). This is a high alcohol, low acid grape with red fruit aromas. The interesting thing about this grape is that it can present some unexpected flavors. While often offering flavors of raspberries and cranberries, there may be undertones of ginger, marzipan, black olives or leather.

While the wines from southern Italy are not as easy to find, they are available and well worth seeking out, as they are often less expensive than the better known wines of Italy. When done well, they can be excellent values.

KEY TO THE WINES OF ITALY

<u>Piedmont</u>
  Nebbiolo
  Barbara
  Moscato

<u>Tuscany</u>
 Sangiovese
 Trebbiano
 Malvasia

<u>Veneto</u>
  Corvina
  Molinara
  Rondinella
  Glera
  Trebbiano
  Pino Grigio

<u>Latinum</u>
  Trebbiano
  Malvasia

<u>Sardinia</u>
 Cannonau

<u>Abruzzo</u>
  Montepulciano

<u>Apulia</u>
 Primitivo

<u>Sicily</u>
  Nero D'Avola
  Catarratto
  Grillo
  Inzolia

Unlike with France, Italian indigenous wine grapes are not exactly "household words."

CHAPTER 4

SPAIN

 **Two things to remember about Spanish wine are:**
1. **Tempranillo (temp rah knee yo) is the signature grape of Spain.**
2. **Sherry is a fortified wine from here.**

Until quite recently, Spain may have been called the slow learner of the wine world. For example, while Spain has the most land cultivated with grape vines, it is only the third largest producer, behind Italy and France, respectively. The main reason for this potential/production discrepancy relates to the fact that most of Spain is a high, flat, dry plateau. Given this parched landscape, it's incredible that restrictions on irrigation weren't fully lifted until 1996!

Also, the *signature* grape of Spain is Tempranillo, which has a flavor profile that is hard to pin down. On top of that, Spanish winemakers traditionally aged their wine in new American oak, with more time in these harshly woody barrels leading to wines with more prestige. It's no wonder that drinking a Spanish wine was often more like chewing on the barrel than drinking its contents!

But the times they are a'changin' *en espanol*. In addition to irrigation, the Spanish have discovered the fruit-preserving benefits of refrigeration, allowing temperature-controlled fermentation. Also, they are moving from long periods of aging their wines to shorter periods in gentler French oak.

Rioja

In north-central Spain along the Ebro River lies Rioja (ree oh ha), the producer of Spain's most prestigious wine, also called just Rioja.

The principal grape in Rioja is Tempranillo, which is called by other names in other parts of Spain, such as Cencibel (sen cee bell), Tinto del Pais (tin toe dale pie ease), Tinto del Toro (toe row) and Tinto Fino (fee know).

Talking Points

- *Isn't it amazing how fruiter Spanish wines are becoming*
- *Tempranillo ripens early and so was named for the Spanish word temprano, which means "early."*
- *It's fascinating that Flor only develops in the Sherry-producing areas of southern Spain.*
- *When the early Sherry-makers first saw Flor, they concluded that that barrel of wine had somehow gotten sick!*
- *Strange that while Sherry here is known as an old lady's wine, it is much appreciated by the macho Spanish bullfighters.*

There will be the squarish Rioja seal on true bottles of Rioja. Rioja bottles may also come surrounded by a thin wire netting. In the past, this wire served to prevent tampering, but it is now only decorative. While Rioja and Tempranillo are a well-known team, this area doesn't have a monopoly on the use of this grape. Wines from Ribera del Duero (ree bear ah del dwar oh), just slightly to the southwest, may also be made from Tempranillo.

Rias Baixas

An exciting white which has burst onto the American wine scene in recent years is Albariño (all bah reen yo). This grape produces a light, citrusy, somewhat "zingy" wine which is good for sipping, particularly in the summer. In the Rias Baixas (ree yahs bike us) wine growing area of Galicia (guh lee cee uh) Province above Portugal, Albariño represents 90% of the grape vines planted.

La Mancha

In the center of Spain is Castilla (ka stee ya), more frequently called La Mancha (mahn cha). This is an area of bulk wine production for thirsty Spaniards across the country, somewhat analogous to Lanquedoc-Roussillon for France and the later-to-be-discussed Central Valley of California.

Catalonia

An up-and-coming wine area of Spain is Priorat (pree oh rat). This area is in northeast Spain, somewhat down the coast from Barcelona. In addition to native Spanish varieties like Garnacha (known in France as Grenache), wines are produced here from Cabernet Sauvignon, giving this prestigious production region a French/Bordeaux twist.

Priorat is in the province of Catalonia (cat ah lone e ah), which over the years has been famous for making sparkling wines. These sparklers are made from native Spanish grapes and not those used in Champagne. They are, however, fermented twice in the same manner as are Champagnes, but they must here be called Cava (cah bah).

Sherry

The most enduring wine of Spain is Sherry. This is a fortified wine produced in the Province of Andalusia (ann duh lu cee a) in extreme southern Spain near the Strait of Gibraltar. Besides Sherry, Andalusia is famous as the home of bullfighting and Flamenco dancing. The name Sherry, by-the-way, is an English corruption of Jerez (hair ez), a port city from which this wine has been shipped.

Sherry begins its life as a dry white wine which is later fortified with a spirit fermented from grapes and then distilled. It may also be sweetened, often by adding sun-dried grapes. Then Sherries are aged in a system of barrels called a Solera (sole air uh).

The Solera is a *fractional blending* system in which Sherries are aged in a succession of barrels. When a portion of the wine is removed from the oldest barrel, it is replaced by wine from the next oldest barrel, which replaced from the next oldest, and on and on until wine is withdrawn from the barrel containing wine that is just newly fermented. This system means that all Sherries contain at least a little wine from the very oldest vintages in the Solera, resulting in wines which always have an aged, mature taste and appearance.

In modern practice, the fortification process determines during the aging process which of two types of Sherries, Fino (fee no) or Oloroso (ole oh row so), a given Sherry will become.

Finos are fortified to only 15.5% alcohol. This rather low level of alcohol allows a yeasty layer to form on the developing Sherries. While, reportedly, disgusting-looking, this Flor (floor) keeps air away from the aging wine. The resulting process of oxygen-free biological aging results in a delicate-tasting wine, thereby earning its name Fino.

Olorosos, on the other hand, are fortified to 17 to 18%. This higher alcohol content prevents Flor from forming, so these Sherries are said to age oxidatively. Olorosos are coarser than Finos, but they can be very appealing, like Cream Sherries, which have been sweetened.

In the course of Sherry service you may also see or hear the terms Manzanilla (man za knee yah), a particularly delicate Fino which may only be aged in the coastal city of Sanlucar de Barrameda (san lou car de bear ah meh dah), Amontillado (ah mon tea ya doe), an aged Fino that develops a rich, nutty taste, and Palo Cortado (pal low core tod oh), which only develops limited Flor and is, thus, intermediate in taste between a Fino and an Oloroso.

True Sherries come only from Spain, and they should not be confused with cheap cooking wines that are, lamentably, sold under that name.

A Key to the Wines of Spain

<u>Galacia/Rias Baixes</u>
Albariño

<u>Catalonia/Cava</u>
Parellada
Xarel-lo
Macabeo

<u>Rioja</u>
Tempranillo

<u>Ribera del Duero</u>
Tempranillo

<u>Priorat</u>
Garnacha

<u>La Mancha (Castilla)</u>
Bulk Wines
Airen (white)
Cencibel (Tempranillo)

<u>Andulucia/Sherry</u>
Palomino
Pedro Ximenez
Moscatel

As with Italy, the names of these grapes aren't exactly household words.

CHAPTER 5

PORTUGAL

Two things to remember about Portuguese wines are:
1. **Most wines from here are made from indigenous grapes which are largely unfamiliar to us.**
2. **Port is a fortified wine from here.**

Portugal is a small, agricultural country which, of course, shares the Iberian Peninsula with Spain. Like Spain, its most prestigious wine is fortified. But there is a basic, fundamental difference between Port and Sherries. Whereas Sherries are, as we've seen, fortified after fermentation, Ports are fortified when the fermentation process is only approximately half completed. In this case, the addition of grape spirits stops the conversion of sugar into alcohol. So the sweetness in Port is from the sugar in the grapes, not added later as in Sherry. In that sense, Port is a *vin doux natural* (ven do nat chew ral), or a naturally sweet wine. We'll discuss the many types of Ports toward the conclusion of this chapter.

Vinho Verde

Vinho Verde (veen yo vaird) literally means green wine. But the green here doesn't relate to color but to being young, as in "greenhorn." As a matter of fact, there are red Vinho Verdes!

These wines are produced in the northern Portuguese province of Minho (meen yo). They may be white, rosé or red, with the whites typically being carbonated. Such spritzy wines from Portugal were popular here in the States a number of years ago, and you may recall the odd-shaped, sometimes ceramic bottles in which they were sold. However, many of these carbonated wines were actually produced further south from Minho.

Douro

The Douro (do row) is the region in which Port is produced. But a limit is set on the percentage of grapes which may be put into the making of this fortified wine, thus encouraging the development of fine Portuguese table wines. This is a red wine area, and the fine wine grapes employed here are Touriga Nacional (tow reeg ah na cee oh nal), Portugal's most prestigious grape, and Tinta Roriz (tin tah row ease), which is actually our friend Tempranillo from across the Spanish border.

Matt Kramer, who writes for *Wine Spectator*, recently praised Portuguese wines, which are largely made from grapes brought to the area in ancient times by the Phoenicians, for their improving quality in the face of still low prices. He points out that, fortunately for the wine industry in this area, the horizontally-laid deposits of schist, a form of rock, have been broken up by seismic activity, allowing grape vine roots to penetrate deep into the soil in search of nutrients.

Bairrada

This region is notable for the fact that its red wines must be at least half composed of the local Baga (baa gah) grape. While 50% is the legal minimum, 80% is actually more typical. White wines are produced in this region from grapes called Maria Gomes (said as it looks but note that there is no "z" as in Gomez) and Bical (bee caul).

Dão

While 75% of the wines from here are red, this is the home to the white grape Arinto (ah reen tow), which is praised as being a refreshing, high-acid grape.

Talking Points

- *Aren't these Portuguese wines amazing, given their quality AND affordability?*
- *Late-bottled Vintage Port has such an impressive name, particularly since it's so much less prestigious than just Vintage Port!*
- *Maderization, the process by which wines darken following being heated, usually considered a flaw, is named after Madeira.*

Port

Port, of course and as noted at the beginning of this chapter, is Portugal's most famous alcoholic beverage. It is produced along the Douro River, which runs from Spain across northern Portugal and into the Atlantic. Interestingly, Ports from the rough, mountainous interior are considered superior to those fortified nearer the coastal cities from which this fortified wine is shipped. It is generally believed that Port developed out of the trade conducted between Portugal and England. Whereas English wool arrived in fine shape, the wine with which it was bought spoiled during the long ocean voyage to the British Isles. The solution was to add brandy to the wine to preserve it. This taste was agreeable to Englishmen, and to this day most Port shippers have very proper Anglo names such as Taylor, Grahams, Cockburn and Churchill, to name a few.

Ports are fortified according to the point to which the sugar content of the must has dropped during the course of the fermentation process, which translates to between six and eight percent alcohol by volume. The final alcohol level in Port is about 20%, and, of course, since fermentation was arrested in the face of a high level of remaining sugar, this is a syrupy sweet wine.

Ports are classified in terms of whether they are aged in barrels or bottles. The main categories that are barrel-aged are:

> Ruby Port
> Tawny Port
> Aged Tawny Port
> Late-Bottled Vintage Port

These wines are ready to drink when purchased and do not throw a sediment.

> Bottle-aged Ports are:
> Vintage Port – These are from a single year which has been declared to be outstanding.

Single Quinta Port – These come from a single property Quinta (keen tah), which means estate in Portuguese.

Bottle-aged Ports tend to improve with age and throw a sediment, requiring *decanting*, as discussed in a later chapter on wine service.

Madeira

Madeira is an island off the coast of Africa, but it is a province of Portugal. Its namesake wine is like Port in the sense that it is often fortified during the fermentation process and is, thus, sweet, but not always. When made from the Italian grape Malvasia or the local grapes Tinta Negra Mole (teen ta neg rah moe lay) or Boal (bo al), it is sweet. When made with Verdelho (ver dell you) or Sercial (sir cee all), a grape with the synonym Esgana Cão (es gah nah cow) which translates to "dog strangler," the Madeira will be dry and, as indicated by the name, rather acidic.

Madeiras have been shipped around the world, including to the British colonies in North America prior to the Revolution. In the course of this extensive shipping, particularly through tropical waters, it was discovered that the wines improved during sea voyages, becoming smoother and more carmelized. Producers of Madeira now simulate such long sea voyages by heating the wine in Estufas (s stu fahs) or, to produce an even higher-quality wine, by storing their wines in the hot attics of their warehouses for years.

A Key to the Wines of Portugal

Vinho Verde
Alvarinho
Trajadura
Loureir
Arinto

Douro/Port
Touriga Nacional
Touriga Franca
Tinta Roriz
Tinta Barroca and more....

Barrada
Baga

Dão
Red

       Touriga Nacional
       Tinta Roriz
White
       Arinto
       Bical
       Encruzado

Madeira
Red
       Tinta Negra Mole
Whites
       Malvasia (AKA Malmsey)
       Baul
       Sercial
       Verdelho

CHAPTER 6

GERMANY

Three things to remember about German wines are:

1. **Germany is cold. It is home to some of the coldest climate vineyards in the world.**
2. **Germany grows a lot of white grapes. According to the Wine Economics Research Center of the University of Adelaide, about 64% of the grapes grown in Germany are white.**
3. **Germany is home to one of the seven noble grapes, and that is the Riesling grape. It is, of course, a white grape.**

Germany is Cold

Because of Germany's cool climate, most of the vineyard land is located in the southwestern part of the country where temperatures are slightly warmer. Most vineyards are also located near a body of water. Water moderates temperatures, keeping the vineyards warmer. The three most important bodies of water to German vineyards are the Rhine River, the Mosel River and Bodensee, also known as Lake Constance. Another factor that helps to keep the vineyards warm enough for grape growing is the soil that is abundant in the Rheingau and Mosel. It is a slate soil that is particularly good at retaining heat.

A Lot of White Grapes

Because white wine grapes are known for their acidity, and greater acidity develops in cool climates, it makes sense that 64% of German grapes grown are white. The red grapes that are grown in Germany are reds that are known for their acidity, the primary one being Pinot Noir, known in Germany as Spätburgunder (shpat bour gunder). Vineyards of Spätburgunder are becoming more prevalent as global warming increases the temperatures of the vineyards.

Riesling

Twenty percent of the grapes grown in Germany are Riesling, one of the seven noble grapes. Considered an aromatic grape, Riesling is high in acidity and low in alcohol, with aromas of peach, nectarine, apricot, honeysuckle, jasmine and baking spices. But the telltale aroma of Riesling is petrol. If your nose is in a white wine, and you think you smell a new basketball, you are smelling a Riesling. While many areas grow Riesling grapes, including Washington State, Clare Valley, Australia and Alsace, France, the grape originated in Germany, and some might argue that Germany grows it best. What makes Riesling a noble grape are its complex aroma profile, good structural elements such as acidity and its ability to age well. Riesling can be cellared for several years, and it will become more complex and interesting as it ages.

In Germany, quality wine is named for the ripeness level of the grapes. For example, if the label has the word "Kabinett" (cob ee net) on it, the wine was made from the earliest-picked of the quality grapes. The earlier a grape is picked, the less sugar concentration it will have. This does not necessarily mean that the wine will not be sweet. If fermented dry, a Kabinett wine will have an alcohol level of 10%. The ripeness ratings are completely objective, based on the measurable sugar content of the grapes. The wonderful thing about the scheme with which German grapes are rated is that once you know how to read the label you will know whether a wine is dry, off-dry or sweet. If the wine is a Kabinett with an alcohol level of eight percent, that is a sweet wine. If it is nine percent, it is off-dry, and if it is ten percent, the wine has been fermented completely dry. All the sugar has been turned into alcohol. The next ripeness level is Spatlese (shpat lay zuh), with a twelve percent alcohol potential. A Spatlese with an alcohol level below twelve percent will be off-dry to sweet, depending on how low the alcohol level is. After Spatlese comes Auslese (ouse lay zuh), which can produce a wine with fourteen percent alcohol when fermented dry. An Auslese Riesling with an alcohol level of fourteen percent will be full-bodied, aromatic and completely dry. An Auslese Riesling with an alcohol level of twelve percent will have quite a bit of residual sugar in it.

There are three more ripeness levels above Auslese, and they are Beerenauslese (bare en ouse lay zuh), Eiswein (ice vine) and Trockenbeerenauslese (trock en bare en ouse lay zuh). The later the grape is picked and the longer it hangs on the vine, the greater its sugar level will be. These grapes are considered *late harvest* grapes. At these levels, the sugar content is high enough that these grapes are generally, although not always, made into dessert wines.

German wines are the only wines that give you this information on the label. It will not work with a Washington State Riesling. But if you are in a store and know that you want a dry German Riesling, look for a 10% Kabinett, 12% Spatlese or 14% Auslese. You will have your dry Riesling. If you want an off-dry or sweet Riesling, look for lower alcohol percentages. You will certainly look like you know what you are talking about when you pick up a bottle of German Auslese Riesling with a 13% alcohol level and state with certainty, "This wine is off-dry. It has some residual sugar." Then you can go on to say, "A good acidic wine like Riesling with some residual sugar is the perfect accompaniment to spicy Asian dishes."

Just to clarify, the terms "Kabinett," "Spatlese" and "Auslese" are used to label the sugar content/ripeness level of the grapes. They are not the producer, type of grape or region. They are just the pre-fermentation ripeness levels.

Aside from Riesling, the second most common grape that is grown in Germany is Müller-Thurgau. It takes up just under 15% of Germany's vineyard area. It is a white grape that is a cross between Riesling and a lesser known grape, Chassalas de Courtillier aka Madleine Royal. Müller-Thurgau was created in the 19th century in order to produce a grape that had the noble qualities of Riesling but that ripened earlier. Though the crossing did not produce a grape with the noble qualities of Riesling, Müller-Thurgau is still the second most grown grape in Germany.

Two other grapes that are commonly grown in Germany are Pinot Gris, which is known as "Grauburgunder" (grou burg under) and Pinot Blanc, which is known as "Weissburgunder" (vice burg under). In smaller quantities, Germany also grows other international varieties, such as Chardonnay and Gewürztraminer. Along with these international varieties, many indigenous varieties are grown.

Unlike most other European countries, with German wines the name of the grape will be on the label if it has been made with at least 85% of that grape variety. Labeling the wine varietally is common in New World countries, such as the US and Australia. But in the Old World, or Europe, most countries label their wines by the region. Because the Old World has such strict laws, once you know the region you will know the variety. In Germany you will find both the region and the variety on the label for single varietal wines.

While a majority of the wine produced in Germany is white and still, the country does make red wines, such as the previously mentioned Pinot Noir. They also make dessert wines from the high ranked grapes in the Beerenauslese and Trockenbeerenauslese levels. And they make a surprising amount of sparkling wine. Rather than using the traditional method for their sparkling wine such as is done in Champagne, Germany uses what is called the tank method. The second fermentation does not take place in the bottle, as with traditional sparkling wine. Instead, the wine is fermented in a tank. It is a more efficient way of making sparkling wine, but it doesn't produce the same small bubbles for which the traditional method is known.

Talking Point

- *Germany has the world's highest per-capita consumption of sparkling wine.*

There are 13 wine regions in Germany. The two that are most commonly seen here in the United States are Mosel and Rheingau. Although these two regions combined only make up about 12% of the wine produced in Germany, they are considered to make the best Rieslings. Both areas have the slate soil that is so important for retaining heat. Both regions plant their vineyards along a river. In Mosel it is the river by the same name. In Rheingau it is the Rhine River. The Rieslings of Mosel are known for their high acidity. The Rieslings of the Rheingau are more full-bodied.

Talking Point

- *You can tell which region a German wine comes from by the color of the bottle. A brown bottle is a Riesling from the Rheingau, Pfaltz or Nahe. A green bottle is a Riesling from Mosel. Both will be "long neck" bottles, that is the long, slender style of bottle.*

No Key to the Wines of Germany?

Because of Germany's identification with one grape, Riesling, which is grown throughout its wine producing areas, the kind of geographical outline which helps one understand the wines of France, Italy, Spain and Portugal is not relevant here.

Austria's identification with Grüner Veltliner is a similar case, in our opinion.

Following this chain of thinking, New World countries are not subject to neat geographical outlines in that, basically, Old World varietals are planted wherever wine producers decide to plant them.

CHAPTER 7

AUSTRIA

One thing to remember about Austrian wine is:

1. Grüner Veltliner (gruh-ner velt lee ner). Grüner Veltliner is a white grape that makes a spicy and full-bodied wine with good acidity.

Grüner Veltliner pairs well with fish, vegetables, especially peas, and cured or smoked meats. A big plate of pasta with shrimp, peas and bacon would be great with a Gruner. While Gruner is grown in other countries, it is done best in Austria, so much so that Grüner Veltliner is known as Austria's grape, making up no less than 30% of all grapes grown. Austria does grow other white varieties, such as Riesling and Müller-Thurgau. Austrian Rieslings are lovely and almost always fermented dry. But Austria is known for its Grüner Veltliner.

The climate of Austria is cool. Most vineyards rely on the moderating effects of a body of water such as the Danube. But because it is not as cool as the vineyards of Germany, Austria is able to grow more red varieties. About 35% of grapes grown in Austria are red. While some international reds are grown, such as Pinot Noir, Merlot and even Cabernet Sauvignon, most of the red grapes grown in Austria are indigenous, that is native to Austria and not grown successfully anywhere else. The three red Austrian wines that you are most likely to find in US stores are St. Laurent (sanct lau rehn), Blaufränkisch (blau frehnk ish) and Zweigelt (tsvy gelt). Zweigelt is a cross between St. Laurent and Blaufränkisch and is the most popular of the three, making up 10% of all grapes grown in Austria. Blaufränkisch has aromas of red fruit and blueberry with some savory flavors. It can be well structured and have good acidity. St. Laurent is related to Pinot Noir. It makes a medium-bodied wine with red fruit aromas. The most popular grape, Zweigelt, makes a wine that is both fruity and peppery. It pairs well with red meats and mushrooms. A grilled pork chop with a mushroom sauce would be its perfect accompaniment.

Talking Points

- *Austria was one of only two countries in Eastern Europe that was able to remain outside of Communist rule in the 20th century. What does*

> *this have to do with wine? Communist rule is one of the factors that halted the wine industry in the 20th century in Eastern Europe. The other factor was World War II.*

- *Austria's vineyards are only in the eastern part of the country because the rest of Austria is covered in mountains (aka the Alps).*

On the eastern side of the country there are three broad wine growing regions. They are Niederosterreich (nee dehr us ter reic), Burgenland (boor gen land) and Steiermark (sty er marc). Within these three broad regions are eight quality regions known as "DACs" (Districtus Austriae Controllatus). You always want to see the letters "DAC' on the wine label to know that you are drinking a quality wine. The best Grüner Veltliner wines come from Kremstal (krem stahl) and Kamptal (kamp tall). The best Zweigelt comes from Neusiedlersee.

Austrian wine laws are similar to those of Germany. As in Germany, Austria ranks its grapes by ripeness level and sugar content. Though there are some differences between the two countries' classification systems, Austria also has Kabinett, Spatlese and Auslese grape level classifications.

Although Austria has a long history of wine-making, the country is a fairly new player in the international wine world. They didn't begin using an appellation system (DAC) until 2003. They also had a big setback in the 1980's when a few Austrian wine brokers were caught artificially adulterating their wines with diethylene glycol. Since then, stricter controls have been put in place, and the DAC wines that are exported are now of top quality.

Talking Point

- *The company that makes those famous wine glasses, the ones that are designed to enhance the flavor of the wine, Riedel (rhymes with needle), is based in Austria.*

THE NEW WORLD

In the *New World,* that is regions outside Europe, winemaking tends to place less emphasis on *terroir* and more on techniques employed in the winery. Perhaps the most consistently used technique is refrigeration/controlled temperature fermentation, which prevents the fruit taste from being "boiled away" during the kinds of extremely high temperature fermentations which can occur during those periodic reappearances of summer weather after the fall harvest. This "fruit-forward" characteristic of New World wines is so well-known that if during a tasting it is remarked that a wine tastes fruitier than it smells, you would get high marks for your conclusion that it is a New World wine.

Another New World technique is "cold-soaking" to increase the body of otherwise thin Pinot Noirs. Fermentation here is delayed so that the juice of the grapes can macerate, that is soak in the grape skins, for a longer period, allowing greater extraction of phenolics and fruit aromas. Longer hang-time is another technique used in New World style wines. The more ripe the grapes become, the greater their sugar content. The higher sugar converts to a higher alcohol content in the wine. Perhaps the most prominent mark of New World wine is the use of new oak. New oak barrels impart a great deal of oak, nuts, vanilla and sometimes chocolate aromas to the wine. Used oak, on the other hand, imparts a much more subtle aroma to the wine.

CHAPTER 8

NORTH AMERICA

The European colonies on the east coast of North America immediately seemed promising as wine-producing areas. After all, the earlier-visiting Norseman had named this continent "Vineland" because of the profusion of grape vines they saw here. However and as we shall see, it took our continent a very long time indeed to live up to this prematurely-assessed potential.

The initial disappointment in attempts at winemaking here related to the fact that native American grapes are of a different subspecies from the European fine wine grapes, that is and as discussed in the introductory chapter, they are <u>not</u> of the *Vitis vinifera* type. Not unexpectedly, the rustic, pungent wines these grapes produce were not to the liking of European settlers. They can, however, become an acquired taste, as we discuss in the sections on Eastern United States wine producing regions.

The colonists responded to this challenge by importing European grape vines, but they quickly died here. In fact, no less an intellect than Thomas Jefferson failed at this noble endeavor. It was at the time thought that the vines had died because of the extremely cold winters of North America. It was, however, later discovered that these disappointments were actually to be blamed on *phylloxera*, the plant louse discussed in the introductory chapter of this work.

The first success in the cultivation of *vinifera* grapes came in the less humid West when Spanish friars began planting and making wine from the *Mission Grape*, also known simply as "The Black Grape." While this grape, reportedly, yields a coarse, uninteresting wine, it was found to be acceptable for sacramental purposes. We will see that California later became the leader in fine wine production in North America, but this was by no means a direct and smooth path for what we now call "The Golden State."

THE UNITED STATES of AMERICA

California

Five things to know about California wine are:

1. California makes 90% of the wine produced in the US.
2. California wine came on to the world stage in 1976 during a competition now referred to as the Judgment of Paris, a competition between French and California wines where two California wines beat out the French wines.
3. Robert Mondavi is considered the father of the modern California wine industry.
4. Napa is known for its Cabernet Sauvignon.
5. While Napa and Sonoma are the state's most famous wine regions, San Joaquin in Central Valley is the state's largest producing region.

Of course, a lot happened between the Mission Days and the 1860s, such as the American Revolution and California being admitted to the United States. But it was during this decade that the beginning steps toward the modern California fine wine industry were taken. These steps were taken by a most unlikely person, a Soldier of Fortune named Agoston Haraszthy. From Hungary, he called himself both "Count" and "Colonel," but research suggests that he actually had no legitimate claim to either title. He did found Buena Vista Winery in Sonoma, which is still in operation today.

What makes him of general interest to us is that he obtained letters of introduction from Lincoln's secretary of State, William Seward, to travel to Europe and bring back cuttings from some of the most highly regarded vineyards of the Old World. These cuttings were used by his winery and others to begin the process of producing quality table wines in California. Haraszthy himself, though, seems to have quickly tired of the demanding routines of viticulture and winemaking and went on to die in some type of armed conflict over precious metal rights in South America.

The evolving California wine industry suffered a number of setbacks during the early Twentieth Century. Prohibition (1920 – 1933) outlawed the making for sale of alcoholic beverages, and the few wineries that survived this period were reduced to selling sacramental wines and blocks of compressed and dried grapes with the warning not to add water and let sit lest an "illegal alcoholic beverage" be produced. Then there was the Great Depression to lessen demand and World War II to divert attention elsewhere.

In the years following World War II, California winemakers produced nondescript jug wines in the warm Central Valley, as well as sweet, fortified wines like imitation "Port." Attaching European names to these completely unrelated American wines, like "Chablis," "Rhine" and "Hearty Burgundy," both confused consumers and infuriated Old World winemakers.

Some, at the time younger, members of wine-producing families argued that their industry should focus instead on quality varietal-labeled wines made farther north, such as in the more challenging climates of Napa and Sonoma. The man who led and came to symbolize this movement throughout his long life (1913 – 2008) was Robert Mondavi.

Today, the United States is the fourth largest producer of wine in the world. It has recently become the largest market for wine in terms of volume sold, although we are only about 34th in per capita consumption. The Federal Tax and Trade Bureau oversees the wine industry in this country. The primary unit of regulation is the "AVA," which stands for American Viticultural Area. Unlike in Europe, there are no standards for grape varietals employed, winemaking techniques or aging. An AVA listed on the label only guarantees that at least 85% of the grapes used in the wine were grown within the boundaries of that AVA. If a grape variety is listed, at least 75% of that wine must be made of that variety, which gives vintners some flexibility in modifying the taste of their products through blending in other varieties.

In cases in which a winery wishes to make a blend containing less than 75% Cabernet Sauvignon, as is true of many Left Bank Bordeaux, there is a group which gives them that option without having to declassify their wines to "Red California Table Wine." This is the Meritage (contraction of the <u>English</u> words "merit" and "heritage") designation. In essence, a Meritage wine is an American attempt to produce a Bordeaux blend.

The above about the undesirability of declassifying one's wines having been said, it is fascinating that Opus One, the Bordeaux blend which resulted from the collaboration of Robert Mondavi and Baron Rothschild, is labeled simply "Red California Table Wine"! The grapes which go into Opus One are grown just across the street from the Robert Mondavi Winery in Oakville.

Looking back specifically at the State of California, the wine industry here was dramatically changed for the better in the 1980s by two very roughly co-occurring events. For years, the wine studies program at the University of California, Davis had been examining the *terroirs* of the different areas of the state and making recommendations as to which grape varieties should be grown where. Unfortunately but of course, the managers of existing vineyards were not in a practical position to take the professors' advice! But it seems that they had, over the years, grown lax in their anti-*phylloxera* precautions, and the nasty little pest reappeared in California vineyards during this decade. The resulting devastation forced producers to uproot their vineyards and replant on American rootstocks. During this process, they were finally able to avail themselves of the research results coming out of UC Davis.

Today, California produces approximately 90% of all the wine made in the United States!

California's "Super AVAs"
The large, general wine-producing areas of California are:

North Coast – The six counties north of San Francisco

Central Coast – These wine areas stretch, roughly, from Santa Cruz down to Santa Barbara.

Southern Coast – Santa Ynez all the way down to San Diego near the border with Mexico are the areas included here.

Central Valley – The areas of the Central Valley around and south of Lodi are included in this Super AVA.

Sierra Foothills – This is a rural, rustic but up-and-coming wine making area in the rugged foothills of the Sierra Nevadas along California's border with the State of Nevada.

North Coast

While most people have never heard the phrase "North Coast Super AVA," this is the most prestigious and talked about wine region in the New World. That's because of two areas which are here – Napa and Sonoma. But Mendocino, Lake, Marin and Solano Counties are also included in this Super AVA.

Napa

Napa Valley is small and thin, stretching about thirty miles north from San Pablo Bay to Mount St. Helena, an extinct volcano. There are places where it's only a mile wide, but the mountains on both sides are also cultivated in vines. Within this narrow area, there is an astonishing diversity of soil types and microclimates. Temperature variations are extreme here, partly because of the fog off the Bay which in early morning fingers its way into Napa's nooks and crannies before retreating in the face of the sun's heat.

Despite its awesome stature in the wine world, this geologically-blessed little part of Earth actually only produces about four percent of the Golden State's wines. But they do have the most panache. In fact, the first California wine to sell for $100.00 a bottle was a Napa Cabernet Sauvignon.

It was also from here that the wines that stunned the world came, a Napa Valley Chardonnay besting a White Burgundy and a Napa Valley Cabernet Sauvignon coming in First Place against a Bordeaux in the 1976 blind tasting in Paris with French judges!

In addition to Cabernet Sauvignon, Napa's premier and signature varietal, wines are also made here from Chardonnay, Sauvignon Blanc, Merlot, Syrah and Zinfandel. Because the southern end of the valley is actually cooler, being closer to the waters of the Bay, than the areas farther north, the Burgundian varietals of Pinot Noir and Chardonnay particularly shine here. Cabernet

Sauvignon, Syrah and Zinfandel have proven to perform more impressively in the northern parts of the Valley.

You will sometimes see bottles of white wine from here labeled "Fumé Blanc." These wines are actually Sauvignon Blancs that have been oaked. This name and method were the ideas of Robert Mondavi to distinguish his wines from the other, non-descript Sauvignon Blancs of the time. Mr. Mondavi did not, though, copyright this name, so others may and do use it. This style of Sauvignon Blanc has proven to be very popular, winning over the years many tasting panel judgments. The name Fumé Blanc was borrowed from the French Sauvignon Blanc-producing commune of Pouilly Fumé in the Loire Valley, but over there the smoky taste comes from the soil not from exposure to wood.

Quality sparkling wines are also made in California. Many of them, in fact, are made in the traditional manner by Champenoise families, a development which began in 1973 when the Champagne House Moet & Chandon established Domaine Chandon in Napa Valley.

Below is presented an overview of some of the most important sub-AVAs within Napa Valley:

Calistoga: The 1973 Chateaux Montelena Chardonnay was Number One in the Paris tasting.

St. Helena

Rutherford

Oakville: This town is home to the innovative Robert Mondavi Winery.

Yountville

Stag's Leap: The Cabernet Sauvignon that won in Paris was made here.

Oak Knoll

Coombsville

Wild Horse Valley

Los Carneros: This AVA is shared with Sonoma. Being cool, Chardonnay and Pinot Noir do very well here.

The mountain AVA's of Napa are Diamond Mountain, Spring Mountain and Mt. Veeder to the west. Running along the east side of the valley are Howell Mountain and Atlas Peak.

The fact that the award-winning Chardonnay, again a Burgundian varietal, came from the northern part of Napa Valley illustrates the difficulty in summarizing New World wines. Another inconsistency is that Zinfandel, usually a warm-weather grape, thrives both in the hot Central Valley around Lodi and in the Sierra Foothills, which experience frigid, snow-covered winters. You see, in the New World wine producers pretty much produce what they want to produce, and there are times when good wines are made in areas where, theoretically, they shouldn't. But, in general, the French Experience is a good guide to what will fare well where. Northern Oregon Pinot Noir is an excellent example here, as discussed in a later section.

Zinfandel is an exception to the Western European origin of *vinifera* grapes used in winemaking in the New World. It is actually Croatian in origin, where it is called Crljenak (meaning "the red one") Kastelanksi. Zinfandel is only extensively planted here in the US and in the boot of the Italian peninsula, where it is called Primitivo.

Sonoma

West across the Mayacamas Mountains from Napa Valley lies Sonoma. Whereas Napa has been yupped beyond recognition as an agricultural area, Sonoma has retained much of its rural, farming atmosphere.

Below are listed the sub-AVA's within Sonoma County:

Pine Mountain/Cloverdale Peak
Rock Pile
Alexander Valley
Dry Creek
Knight's Valley
Fort Ross/Seaview
Sonoma Coast
Russian River
Green Valley
Bennett Valley
Sonoma Mountain
Valley of the Moon
Sonoma Valley
Los Carneros

Because of the water-related coolness in place here, Russian River is a big producer of Pinot Noir. But there they use various techniques, like cold soaking and whole berry fermentation, to make their wines bigger, fuller, less typically Burgundian. In fact, some Russian River Pinot Noirs actually taste a lot like cherry pop! Green Valley is considered to be a very prestigious sub-area within the Russian River AVA.

The main white grape of Sonoma is Chardonnay. In addition to Pinot Noir, Zinfandel, Syrah and Cabernet Sauvignon are extensively planted here.

Mendocino

Historically, jug wines were produced in the warmer areas here, but the varietals Zinfandel and Petite Sirah are now coming forward.

Petite Sirah (sometimes "Syrah," like the other grape) is an interesting varietal for consideration. *Petite* does, indeed, mean "small." From this you might reasonably assume that Petite Sirah would be a mild, gentler kind of Syrah. But that assumption would be wrong! You see, the convention in the wine world is that size indicators (*piccolo* v. *grosso* as the Italians use these terms with respect to their Sangiovese) refer to the size of the grape, not the substance of the resulting wine. And if you think about it, small grape size means a larger skin-to-juice ratio, producing bigger, more tannic wines. So it is with Petite Sirah. In southern France it is known as Durif (duhr reef), a cross between Peloursin (puh lure seen) and Syrah.

Lake County

This wine-producing area is named in honor of Crystal Lake, which is surrounded by AVAs. The best-known wine area here is Guenoc Valley. The English actress Lillie Langtry used to own a vineyard here, and her lovely portrait continues to be on the label of the Guenoc Winery.

Lake County used to provide grapes for shipment down to the wineries in Napa and Sonoma, but it is increasingly bottling its own wines at home. This is a warm growing area which specializes in Cabernet Sauvignon, Merlot, Zinfandel, Syrah, Petite Sirah and, in an increasing trend in this part of the French-dominated New World wine industry, the Italian-Chianti base grape Sangiovese.

Central Coast

Monterey

A number of well-known wine areas are here, including:

Santa Lucia Highlands: Known for high-altitude Chardonnays, Cabernet Sauvignons and Cabernet Francs

Chalone: Broad temperature swings here bring out the best in Pinot Noirs and Chardonnays.

Arroyo Seco: Known for its gravel soil and age-worthy reds

San Lucas: Bordeaux varietals plus Chardonnay

Hames Valley: Bordeaux wines

San Antonio Valley: This is basically a warm area, but it is cooled by ocean breezes.

Cabernets and Zinfandels from here are well-regarded.

Carmel: Bordeaux varietals are planted on ridges here.

Paso Robles

Paso, as it is called by wine buffs, is actually one of the oldest viticultural areas in California. It has been reasserting itself over the past decade or so, and the wine industry here has grown dramatically. It is probably the warmest AVA in California, but it enjoys the cool nights needed to produce balancing acidity. Zinfandel does very well here, accordingly. A really exciting development here has been the use of Rhône varietals by a dedicated group of winemakers. The varying terroirs of Paso Robles are still being discovered. In late 2014, eleven new AVA's were approved within the county.

Talking Points

- *It's so amusing to hear people pronounce Meritage with a French accent!*
- *I think it's a fascinating blend of French and Western traditions that the vintners of California's Paso Robles AVA who are using Rhône varietals call themselves the "Rhône Rangers"!*
- *It's interesting that while most varietals run out of steam at about 20 years, Zinfandel vines can produce good wines for decades longer.*
- *Oregon's success with Pinot Noir is a classic New World wine story in which the discovery of similar terroirs to those utilized successfully over time in France lead to wonderful wines.*
- *It's interesting that while in Europe "Reserve" relates to aging requirements, it's more of a general quality designation in Washington State.*

Edna Valley

This area is south of Paso and is cooler because of the ocean's influence here. It is responsible for good value varietals, particularly its Chardonnays and Pinot Noirs.

Santa Barbara

Unlike in most parts of California, the valleys here run west to east, facilitating the cooling effects of the ocean. The main AVAs here are:

Santa Maria Valley
Happy Canyon
Santa Ynez Valley

Santa Rita Hills

Santa Barbara specializes in wines made from Sauvignon Blanc, Chardonnay, Pinot Noir, Syrah and Merlot.

Southern Coast

You rarely have an opportunity to sample wines from Southern California, the industry here being increasingly severely restricted by urban sprawl. The most successful remaining wineries are in the Temecula area around Riverside. Their success appears to be largely attributable to the fact that cooling ocean breezes come into the area through Rainbow Gap. Fittingly for a warm growing area, the Mediterranean variety Sangiovese is used here, in addition to some of the "standard' French varietals.

Central Valley

The Central Valley is, of course, the huge agricultural area for the State of California. Historically, therefore, it has been know for the bulk production of *jug wines*. However, the Robert Mondavi Woodbridge Winery is located here, and they produce solid wines at affordable prices for daily consumption. The area around Lodi, additionally, has earned prestige for its Zinfandels.

Sierra Foothills

This Super AVA consists of eight counties in Eastern California, of which the two most important are El Dorado and Amador. The wine industry in this rugged region was founded by Italian immigrants who, unlike their more "gentrified" fellow countrymen in Napa, have for some time planted Italian varietals here. But this region is actually best known for its Old Vine Zinfandels. While "old vine" has no legal definition, these vines do, indeed, tend to be old, many at 40 plus years. They are often put into stout blends with Old West names like "Hangtown Red."

Oregon

One thing to remember about Oregon wine is: Pinot Noir!

A man named David Lett is called "Papa Pinot" here. He had spent time in Burgundy and had picked up their "no pain, no gain" philosophy of winemaking. Upon coming home, he found that McMinnville, Oregon in the Willamette Valley in the north-western part of the state had similar daily rainfall, temperatures and hours of sunlight to Beaune in Burgundy. Hence, he reasoned successfully, the great Burgundian red should do well here too.

And Papa Pinot was successful in spades! In a blind tasting held in Paris in 1979, Lett's Eyrie Vineyards did well in a competition including Burgundies. Robert Drouhin of the prominent Burgundian wine family thought these results might have been a fluke, so he repeated the tasting. This time the Eyrie Pinot Noir placed toward the top again! Convinced now, Monsieur Drouhin purchased a vineyard near Lett's where his daughter Veronique is the winemaker.

In one of the first major departures from the "white with white and red with red" rule, it was discovered that Pinot Noir is an ideal accompaniment to the salmon caught off the Oregon Coast. This taste harmony results from the fact that for a red, Pinot Noir is low in tannins. A tannic wine, like Cabernet Sauvignon, gives fish a metallic taste.

Consistent with what you would expect, whereas Pinot Noir does well in the north of Oregon, Bordeaux varieties like Cabernet Sauvignon and Merlot perform well in the warmer Rogue Valley to the south and in Walla Walla in the interior.

Pinot Gris is an up-and-coming white varietal here in Oregon.

Washington

Two things to remember about Washington are:
1. **The vineyards are actually east of the Cascades, in the desert portion of the otherwise "Evergreen State."**
2. **And Merlot is the breakout grape of the state.**

Agriculture in a desert must, of necessity, rely on irrigation, which is readily available here. Actually, there are advantages to watering that way in that the winemaker can control the amount of water received by the vines. Research from the experimental wine program at the University of Nevada, Reno shows that some grape varieties produce more flavorful wines when they have been *drought stressed*.

Another advantage to this vineyard placement is that the sandy desert soils are not hospitable to *phylloxera*, so this nasty little pest has never been a problem here. Washington's grapevines have never had to be grafted onto American rootstocks. Many wine fanciers feel that this complete *vinifera* type of growth leads to a more authentic wine, but this has never been conclusively demonstrated.

Washington State is the nation's second largest producer of *vinifera* grapes, obviously behind California. The largest producer of wine in this state is Yakima Valley, roughly in the middle of the state. There are about 60 wineries here, making close to a third of Washington's wines. Washington is the only New World jurisdiction to set a legal meaning for the frequently seen term "Reserve." Here it means no more than ten percent of a producer's yearly output and no more than 3,000 cases.

Washington State, being so far north, has cool nights and long hours of sunlight during the day. This pattern leads to long *hang times* for the grapes, helping to produce the fruity, jammy Merlots for which the state is so justly famous. Not unexpectedly, German varietals, such as Riesling, also do very well up here.

New York

New York is actually the US's second largest producer of wine, but much of its wines are fermented from native American grapes. These *foxy* wines continue to be made in the Finger Lakes region in the middle of New York, and they are enjoyed by people who grew up drinking them.

Konstantin Frank disputed the then accepted wisdom that the climate in New York was too cold for the growth of *vinifera* grapes. He knew better because of his involvement in the successful cultivation of *vinifera* grapes in his native Russia. Dr. Frank, thus, became the father of the *vinifera* wine industry in the Eastern United States.

The Chardonnays and Rieslings made here tend to be lighter and crisper than those from California or even Europe. While most New York wines are white, red Bordeaux varietals are increasingly being planted in the state. The North Fork of Long Island, obviously also a maritime environment, is a developing area for the production of such Bordeaux varietal wines.

Eisweins, made in the German fashion, are a particularly prized vinous product of the State of New York.

Other States

Arizona – There are ten irrigated wineries here. Coyotes are a problem as they like both grapes and the essential irrigation hoses.

Missouri – The first AVA was actually here – Augusta in 1980!

Nevada – There are commercial wineries here, and the Pinot Noirs produced by the University of Nevada, Reno experimental wine program are surprisingly Burgundian.

New Mexico – Gruet, a sparkling wine made by people from France, made *Wine Spectator's* Top 100 Wines of the Year.

Ohio – Making wine since its statehood in 1803, Ohio is now home to 215 wineries.

Pennsylvania – Burgundy-type wines are produced here.

Rhode Island – They produce wines from cool climate grapes like Gewurztraminer, Chardonnay and Pinot Noir. The French-American hybrid Vidal Blanc does well here.

Texas - Mediterranean varietals are on the rise in the Lone Star State.

Virginia – Hybrids (*vinifera* x native grape crossings) and native American varietals make up almost a fourth of wine production here. Norton is a red American grape used to make Virginia Claret, which somewhat resembles

Zinfandel in taste. Horton's Norton is a famous Virginia Claret. Virginia is also developing a reputation for the southern Rhône white grape Viognier.

Every state in the union now produces wine. As wine technology continues to improve, the state wine industries will continue to grow. We encourage you to explore the wines of your state.

CANADA

Canada, naturally, specializes in cold-climate grapes like Chardonnay and Riesling. Major wine-producing areas are on Vancouver Island and the Okanagan Valley, and in the eastern part of the country in Ontario on the Niagara Peninsula and along the north shore of Lake Erie. Canadian ice wines are highly regarded. In fact, our northern neighbor has entered into a treaty with Germany and Austria under which ice wines may only be made in the traditional way, with the grapes fully fermented outside in winter. By law, the grapes must be picked at 17.6 degrees Fahrenheit or lower. Even with these stringent standards in place, Canada makes the most ice wine in the world!

MEXICO

The primary wine-making area of Mexico is in Baja California, specifically the Guadalupe Valley. While you will seldom taste a Mexican wine, they are mostly reds from Cabernet Sauvignon, Grenache, Syrah and other warm-weather grapes.

CHAPTER 9

ARGENTINA

Six things to remember about Argentinian wine are:

1. Argentina is the world's fifth largest wine producer, coming in behind France, Italy, Spain and the United States.
2. Argentina's signature red grape is Malbec, a grape that originated in Bordeaux, France.
3. Argentina's signature white grape is Torrontés (tore ron tess).
4. There is one region of Argentina that accounts for 70% of the country's vineyard acreage, and that is Mendoza.
5. Nicholas Catena is considered the "godfather" of Argentine wines.
6. Argentina did not become a fine wine producer until the 1990's, largely through the work of Catena.

The vineyards of Argentina are located in the western part of the country, in the foothills of the Andes. Because of the rain shadow effect, as in Alsace, France, Washington State and the South Island of New Zealand, the climate of the wine growing region of Argentina is very sunny and very dry. The rain shadow effect, you may recall, occurs when the air cools as it moves higher in altitude up the mountain. When it reaches a high enough altitude and low enough temperature, the air hits its dew point, releasing its precipitation in the mountains. Thus, the air going to the east side of the mountains, where the vineyards lie, is dry. As that dry air goes down the mountains, decreasing in altitude, it warms up, creating warm and dry conditions for the vineyards east of the mountains. Couple that with the bountiful snow melt from the mountains that is available for irrigation, and you have perfect conditions for growing grapes. The dry climate prevents problems that European climates have, such as mold, fungus and pests. The lack of moisture is ideal for the thin-skinned Malbec grape. Irrigation allows more control over the amount of water a vineyard receives. As research has shown, drought-stressed vines produce more flavorful wines. Such are the conditions in the vineyards of Argentina.

Two very stylish wines are coming out of Argentina right now. One is the red Malbec wine. Originally from the Bordeaux region of France and still grown there as one of the allowable grapes for the Bordeaux blend, Malbec is also grown in Cahors of France and in the Loire Valley, but it does quite well, some would argue even better, in the dry sunny climate of Argentina.

Nicola Catena from Marches, Italy planted his first Malbec vineyard in the early part of the 20th century. But it was actually Nicola's grandson, Nicholas Catena Zapata, who made Malbec the signature grape of Argentina. Considered the "godfather" of Argentine wine, Nicholas, inspired by California's investment into quality wine that was going on in the 1970's and 1980's, felt that he could do the same for Argentina. He planted Cabernet Sauvignon and Chardonnay vineyards and began to produce only quality wines. But his greatest achievement was planting his Malbec vineyards at high altitudes and then using those grapes to produce a fine varietal wine. Nicholas' work is largely responsible for both the quality wines that are coming out of Argentina today and for putting Malbec on the world stage as Argentina's signature grape.

Malbec wine has aromas of dark fruit, spices and violets. It has firm tannins and when planted at higher altitudes as are found in Argentina, displays a good acidity. There are many good Malbecs coming out of Mendoza.

Talking Points

- *A good, spicy, tannic Malbec goes really well with hamburgers, steaks and any grilled beef.*
- *It is said that in Argentina they don't pair their wine with food. They pair their wine with beef.*
- *Torrontés pairs well with seafood and spicy Thai food. It is the young wines that have the best fresh fruit aromas.*

The other stylish wine coming out of Argentina is the white wine Torrontés. Aromatic, spicy and floral, there are at least three clones of the Torrontés grape being grown in Argentina. They are all related to the Muscat grape. It has a medium acidity and is a wine that is not meant to be aged. Drink it young, within one or two years of harvest.

These two trendy wines, Malbec and Torrontés, may be quite popular, but they do not make up the majority of wine production in Argentina. The leading reds coming out of Argentina, those that have the greatest vineyard presence and production, are Cabernet Sauvignon and Syrah. Both with dark fruit aromas and big tannins, these Argentine wines are not always as elegant and nuanced as the same-grape wines of France. But Argentina can provide the right amount of sunshine and warmth, along with some of the world's highest vineyards, to turn out some very impressive, big-bodied, fruit-forward reds that give Argentina its reputation for quality wines.

The leading white wine of Argentina, the one with the greatest vineyard presence and production, is Chardonnay.

While the flavors of this grape can vary from orchard fruits to tropical fruits depending on the climate in which it is planted, the best Chardonnays of Argentina are planted at higher altitudes, producing a more acidic wine with aromas of apple and pear. Much of the Chardonnay that is grown in Argentina is used to produce sparkling wine.

Within Argentina there are eight wine growing regions, all in the western part of the country along the foothills of the Andes. The most productive region in Argentina is Mendoza, accounting for 70% of the country's vineyard area. Mendoza is known for its Malbecs and Cabernet Sauvignons as well as its Torrontés and Chardonnays.

Another notable region of Argentina is Salta. Located north of Mendoza, Salta has some of the highest altitude vineyards in the world, growing grapes at 7000 feet above sea level. This high altitude gives the Salta grapes a very crisp acidity. Salta is best known for its Torrontés.

Talking Points

- *Some of the vineyards of Argentina are as far south as Patagonia.*
- *Although Argentina has been producing wines for centuries, it, up until recently, only produced inexpensive table wines, mainly from the original grape varieties that the Spanish missionaries brought over in the 16th century. It was not until the 1990's that Argentina began focusing its efforts on producing quality wines from quality grapes, such as Malbec, Torrontés, Cabernet Sauvignon, Syrah and Chardonnay.*
- *One negative condition of the Argentine climate, especially in Mendoza, is the frequency of hail storms.*

Because of this, vineyard managers cover their vines with nets to catch the hail stones – "la piedra." They also trellis the vines up high and often vertically in order to prevent hail damage to the fruit resulting when the hail bounces back from the ground, inflicting further destruction on the vines.

- *A lesser known but well done grape in Argentina is a red grape called "Bonarda." Possibly related to the Dolcetto grape of Italy or the Charbono grape of California, Bonarda has red berry aromas and good acidity. In warm climates it can make a fine quality wine, and it is poised to become quite trendy.*

CHAPTER 10

CHILE

Five things to remember about Chilean wine are:

1. Chile is the number one exporter of wine in South America. They export two thirds of their production.

2. Chile has a Mediterranean climate in part due to the Humboldt Current, an ocean current that flows up from the polar seas, bringing with it cool air.

3. The signature grape of Chile is Carmenere (car men air eh), the lost grape of Bordeaux.

4. Eighty percent of the grapes grown in Chile are grown in the Valle Central.

5. Chile is also known for its Chardonnay, 25% of which is grown in Casablanca.

Chile has a beautiful climate in which to grow grapes. It is a long, narrow strip of land that is bordered on the east side by the Andes mountain range and on the west side by the Pacific Ocean. These natural boundaries make Chile somewhat isolated, which is partly the reason why the country has never suffered the scourge of *phylloxera*, a root louse that has devastated most vineyards around the World, either at the end of the 19th century or in the latter part of the 20th century. A second reason that Chile has not been affected by *phylloxera* is that it has sandy soils which are not hospitable to the louse. For both these reasons, Chile is one of the few places in the world that can grow grapes on *Vitis vinifera* rootstock. Most other countries graft their *vinifera* vines onto North American rootstocks which are impervious to *phylloxera*. Is there a difference between the flavors of a wine made from grapes grown on *vinifera* rootstocks and a wine from grafted vines? Possibly. What is certain is that the wines that Thomas Jefferson drank were made before the first great *phylloxera* outbreak and, therefore, were from *vinifera* rootstock grapes. A Bordeaux blend from Chile may quite possibly taste more similar to the wines that were drunk by our forefathers. Although there are too many variables to truly determine whether or not this is true, it certainly is an intriguing idea.

The Valle Central (Central Valley) of Chile, the primary growing region of the country, is just three degrees south of the Atacama Desert, one of the driest places on earth. Yet, the climate of the Valle Central is Mediterranean. This warm, dry, sunny climate with moderate temperatures is largely created by the Humboldt Current, an ocean current that comes up from Antarctica and its cold polar waters. The winds from the Humboldt bring cool air to the Chilean coast. The coastal hills block the moisture in the air, creating the dry, moderate, sunny, Mediterranean climate that the Valle Central enjoys.

Chile is the second largest producer of wine in South America. However, their wine consumption is less than that of their neighbor on the other side of the Andes, Argentina. Consequently, Chile exports a great deal of the wine it produces, as much as 67%. A lot of that wine is exported to the United States, which means that you, dear reader, will have no problems finding Chilean wines on store shelves. This is especially good news because Chilean wine can be some of the best value wines to buy. They have been making wine for centuries and have incorporated a great deal of French influence into their wine making. Many of the famous red grapes, such as Cabernet Sauvignon, Merlot and Syrah, do quite well in the lovely Mediterranean climate of Chile. But because Chile is still somewhat of an "up and coming" region in terms of wine, many of these bold reds can be had for a very reasonable price.

Chile is known for its big, flavorful, fruit-forward red wines. The number one red grape in Chile in terms of plantings is Cabernet Sauvignon, brought over from Bordeaux in the 19th century. The same 19th century Chilean landowners who traveled to France and brought back Cabernet Sauvignon to plant also brought back Merlot, Chile's current number two red grape. What they didn't realize at the time was that they also brought back a third Bordeaux grape that they thought was also Merlot. It wasn't Merlot but actually Carmenere, which is today Chile's third most planted red grape.

Before *phylloxera* struck, wiping out the majority of Europe's vineyards, Bordeaux was planted with the red grapes Cabernet Sauvignon, Merlot, Cabernet Franc, Malbec, Petite Verdot and Carmenere. After *phylloxera* struck, all the grapes were replanted except one - Carmenere. It was believed to have been completely wiped out by the root louse, eradicated forever from the face of the earth. However, those who believed that were wrong. It wasn't until the 1990's when genetic testing was done on the grapes of Chile that people realized that some of what they thought they had planted as Merlot was actually the long lost grape of France, Carmenere. Today it is the signature grape of Chile, enjoying a re-birth in a second home.

Carmenere is a low acid grape. Grown in the Mediterranean climate of Chile, it takes on dark fruit aromas with spice and often earthy aromas such as coffee. The tannins of the wine are soft and round. Carmenere is a very approachable wine with loads of flavor. It pairs well with grilled beef, pork and game. Because of its low acidity, it does not pair well with spicy foods but does go nicely with fruit sauces and herb seasonings.

The number one white grape grown in Chile is Chardonnay. Twenty-five percent of the Chardonnay plantings are in the Casablanca Valley, an area north of the Valle Central and on the coast, where it enjoys cool temperatures from the ocean breezes. This cooler climate produces a crisp wine that offers orchard fruit aromas, such as apple and pear along with some citrus flavors.

Chile's second most prevalent white grape is Sauvignon Blanc, which is grown in the Valle Central, as well as the coastal region of Casablanca. As with Chardonnay, the cool climate of Casablanca produces a very crisp, acidic Sauvignon Blanc.

Chile is a New World wine region. Although there is a long history of grape growing and wine making in the country going back to the 16th century, the modern wines that we know today have only been a part of Chile's wine culture since the 1980's. They are still experimenting and learning what grapes grow well in what regions. Along the way, some great grape to *terroir* matches have been found, such as Chardonnay in Casablanca and Carmenere in the Valle Central. You will, fortunately, find top quality wines coming out of Chile at very reasonable prices.

CHAPTER 11

AUSTRALIA

 Seven things to remember about Australian wine are:

1. Australians call "Syrah" "Shiraz." It is the same grape.
2. Australia is the fourth largest exporter and seventh largest producer of wine in the world.

3. The majority of Australia's wine is made in the southern half of the country. The northern half is too hot.
4. Australia grows a lot of white grapes.
5. In Australia Muscat goes by the name *Gordo Blanco.*
6. In Australia dessert wines are called "stickies."
7. Tasmania is becoming known for its sparkling wines

Although Australia is a New World wine region, it has been making European style wines for over 200 years, longer than the United States. European vines were first brought to Australia at the end of the 18th century. Like the United States, Australia makes big bodied, fruit-forward wines. These qualities reflect the climate as much as a style. In Australia, as in the United States, the climate is warmer than in European countries. The warm climate produces riper grapes. Riper grapes produce wines with more alcohol and more fruit aromas. But that isn't the only similarity that Australia has with the United States. In both countries, up until the middle of the last century the wines that were produced were generally sweet and/or inexpensive bulk wines. It was after the War in the 1940's in the US and the 1960's in Australia that the wine making industry began to take itself seriously enough to focus on quality wines that could compete with the fine wines of Europe.

Though grapes are grown in all regions of Australia, its most productive vineyards are in the southeastern part of the country, in the states of South Australia, New South Wales, Queensland, Victoria and Tasmania. North of these regions temperatures get quite warm, and the grapes lose some of their structure and acidity. South Australia is the region most often named on labels imported to the US. In both South Australia and Victoria, the best growing areas are near the south coast where, because of the maritime climate, temperatures are cooler. In New South Wales the best growing regions are near the Great Dividing Range where the grapes are planted at high altitudes, providing cooler temperatures. Tasmania is surrounded by the frigid Southern Ocean with vineyards near the coast of the island.

In Western Australia, fine wines are coming from the Margaret River area which is south of Perth. It is cooler because of the maritime influence.

Shiraz is grown further inland in regions such as Barossa and McLaren Vale where temperatures are warmer. Australian Shiraz (aka Syrah) is bold, tannic, full-bodied and very fruit-forward. They are strong, intense, flavorful wines that stand up to big meaty meals. As with many of the wines of Australia, Shiraz is often blended with other grapes, both red and white. While Australia is especially known for its big bold Shiraz wines, there are many other grapes grown and types of wines made in the country.

The other big reds for which Australia is known are Cabernet Sauvignon and Merlot, Bordeaux's most famous red grapes. Often, Australian wine makers will blend the grapes rather than produce a varietal wine. However, the wine labels will tell you exactly what you are drinking. The front label will name the grapes used in the wine. The first grape named will be the dominant grape of the blend. The other grapes will be hyphenated after that grape's name in descending order. For example, "Cabernet Sauvignon-Syrah-Merlot" lets you know that the largest portion of the blend is Cabernet Sauvignon, the second most prevalent grape in the blend is Syrah and the smallest amount used is Merlot.

In lesser amounts, Australia also makes Mouvedre and Grenache, both from the Rhône region of France, as is Syrah. And there is some output of the great Burgundian grape Pinot Noir.

The number one white grape produced in Australia, just like in the United States, is Chardonnay. It is grown in both cool and warm climates for the acidic Chardonnays and the tropical fruit Chardonnays, respectively.

Australia is also known for its Sauvignon Blanc, a grape originally from Bordeaux. The Margaret River region in Western Australia is producing some impressive Australian Sauvignon Blanc wines. While that grape is commonly grown in the US, Bordeaux's other white grape, Semillon, is not. It is, however, very popular in Australia, where it is produced as a dry wine as well as a sweet dessert wine. A Semillon from the Hunter Valley of Australia in New South Wales' Great Dividing Range region is lush and full-bodied and can be aged for years, developing even greater depth and complexity.

Germany's noble white grape, Riesling, has long been established in Australia. Great dry Rieslings are from the Clare Valley and Eden in the South Australia State. Sweet, botrytised dessert Rieslings are made in Rutherglen in Victoria.

Other sweet, dessert wines that are quite popular in Australia and also made in Victoria are late harvest, fortified Muscat wines. Muscat is known as Gordo Blanco in Australia. Both of these lush dessert wines are referred to as "stickies" in Australia.

Another wine for which Australia is known is sparkling wine. Along the coast of Tasmania, as well as along the coast of Victoria, vineyards of Pinot Noir and Chardonnay are grown and used to make sparkling wine. Australia also makes a sweet, sparkling wine out of Shiraz grapes that is traditionally enjoyed at Christmas.

Australia is not without its bulk wine industry. Riverland in South Australia produces the largest volume of wine. Murray Darling, a region that straddles both Victoria and New South Wales, also produces bulk table wines. Together with the New South Wales region of Riverina, these three regions produce 50% of Australia's wines. These are not, however, the wines you will want to look for in stores and on restaurant menus. Just as California has its bulk wine region, the Central Valley that makes up 50% of California wine production, so too does Australia have its bulk wine regions. Just like in California, the more interesting wines come from regions outside of the bulk areas.

Talking Points

- *Australians first began calling Syrah "Shiraz" because it was believed that the grape originated in Shiraz, Persia. That has turned out to not be the case, but the name stuck.*
- *The only other country that calls Syrah "Shiraz" is South Africa.*
- *Australia is one of the few places that makes a sparkling Shiraz.*
- *Coonawarra is one of five regions in the Limestone Coast of South Australia. It is renowned for its Terra Rosa soils and its Cabernet Sauvignon wines.*
- *Western Australia is notable in that while it produces only about 10% of the country's wines, it is responsible for a full third of its quality vinous offerings.*

CHAPTER 12

NEW ZEALAND

Three things to remember about New Zealand Wine are:

1. The vineyards of New Zealand are generally cool because of the cold ocean waters that surround the country.
2. New Zealand's two best grapes, the wines for which the country is known, are Pinot Noir and Sauvignon Blanc.
3. Only 15% of the grapes grown in New Zealand are red grapes. Eighty five percent are white.

Though they are often lumped together geographically, New Zealand is actually 1200 miles away from Australia. This distance is enough to put New Zealand well into the cold ocean waters that flow from Antarctica, making the vineyards here perfect for cool-climate grapes such as Sauvignon Blanc and Pinot Noir.

New Zealand also benefits from the rain shadow effect. The climate east of the mountain range on the South Island, the Southern Alps, is sunny and dry, as the mountains block the rain clouds. The combination of cool temperatures, sunshine and dry air produces grapes with a good acid/sugar balance.

Seventy five percent of new plantings in New Zealand are of either Sauvignon Blanc or Pinot Noir. These are the two grapes that are making a name for the country in the world of fine wine. While the two varieties are grown on both islands of the country, it is on the cooler South Island where the majority of the vineyards for these two grapes lie. Specifically, 60% of all Sauvignon Blanc and Pinot Noir vines are in Marlborough on the northern tip of the South Island.

Pinot Noir from New Zealand has red fruit aromas and good acidity. It is generally less earthy than Pinot Noir from Burgundy, France. Sauvignon Blanc, a variety that is known to vary greatly in response to its *terroir*, takes on aromas of stone fruit, grapefruit and grass in the cool climate of New Zealand.

On the North Island, especially in the regions of Hawke's Bay and Gisborne where the temperatures are higher, more warm-weather grapes, such as Cabernet Sauvignon, Merlot and Syrah, are grown. New Zealand also produces Chardonnay, Pinot Gris and Riesling. But, again, the wines to watch from New Zealand are Pinot Noir and Sauvignon Blanc.

Talking Points

- *You can tell a Sauvignon Blanc from New Zealand by its grassy and grapefruit aromas and bright acidity.*
- *The cool climate of New Zealand's South Island creates acidic grapes that make the wine very food-friendly.*
- *Gisborne has dubbed itself the Chardonnay capital.*

CHAPTER 13

SOUTH AFRICA

 Four things to remember about South African wines are:

1. South Africa is the only country in the world with a wine region influenced by two oceans, the Atlantic and the Indian.

2. **South Africa has, until recently, been the "hard luck kid" of the wine world, having been restricted by a powerful wine cartel and then having its wines boycotted by other countries in protest to the racial policy of Apartheid.**
3. **Pinotage (pea no tagze) is the signature grape of South Africa.**
4. **Chenin Blanc is called "Steen" here.**

Since the end of Apartheid in 1991, the South African wine industry has made great strides. The idea-poor cartel called the KWV (which stands for seven hard-to-pronounce Dutch words - Kooperatieve Wijinbouwers Verenigin van Zvid-Afrika Bpkt - See, we told ya to fergitaboutit!) has been reduced to controlling only about 25% of the nation's output. There is more emphasis being placed on red varietals and less on whites like Steen. Pinotage, a cross of Pinot Noir and Cinsault, created at Stellenbosch University in 1925, is being less employed in favor of international varieties like Cabernet Sauvignon and Shiraz. Yes, the South African spell it just like the Aussies. But the most important improvement is that it is now politically and socially acceptable to serve South African wines. Indeed, members of the Mandela family have entered the wine business here.

Talking Points

- *Pinotage is a contraction of the names Pinot Noir and Hermitage, which is what the South Africans called Cinsault. That's ironic in that Hermitage is an appellation in the Northern Rhône, whereas Cinsault is a blending grape in the Southern Rhone.*

- *At its best Pinotage, produces a zesty red wine kind of like Zinfandel. But some complain of a subtle paint-like smell, which has somewhat diminished international enthusiasm for this vinifera cross.*
- *Baboons are a unique threat to wine grapes in South Africa. And because they're so intelligent, they are difficult to thwart. One "technique" that has proven to be dramatically ineffective against these invaders is throwing rocks at them. You guessed it, the baboons throw them back at you!*

The great bulk, 95%, of the vineyards of South Africa are located in the southwestern part of this country, in the Western Cape along the coast. The climate here is made more temperate than it would otherwise be by the influence of the Benguela Current, which brings cold water up from Antarctica.

The first success for the South African wine industry occurred on the peninsula called Constantia where a sweet wine made from the Muscat grape, called "Hanepoot" here, was produced. It was said to have been a favorite of no less than Napoleon Bonaparte himself.

South Africa uses the *Wine of Origin* (WO) scheme for maintaining quality standards, which is roughly equivalent to our *American Viticultural Area* framework. A white band across the capsule signifies certification by the South African Wine and Spirit Board.

Pinotage may be combined with international varieties like Cabernet Sauvignon and Shiraz to make *Cape Blends.*

Overall, however, the South Africans are forsaking sweet, fortified and Pinotage-based wines for standard art-exhibit-opening varietals like Sauvignon Blanc and Chardonnay on the white side and Cabernet Sauvignon,

Merlot, Shiraz and Pinot Noir on the red. However and additionally, they are using the white Colombard, used for bulk wine production in our Central Valley, and the French red blending grapes of Cabernet Franc and Grenache.

The Breede River Valley, which includes both Robertson and Worchester, is the most productive area of South Africa, with over a third of all the country's wines hailing from here. In fact, twenty-five percent of the country's wines come from Worchester alone, but they are mostly of the bulk type.

A particularly high-quality wine area of South Africa is the Overberg District, the wine region where the Atlantic and the Indian Oceans meet. Their combined maritime influences make this a cool area and, thus, favorable for Chardonnay and Pinot Noir, especially at Walker Bay, which has recently become its own WO. The Elgin Ward here is slightly higher in elevation and is gaining a reputation for its Sauvignon Blancs.

Most other countries in Africa are too hot and arid for wine production and/or and are dominated by religious traditions unsympathetic to drinking alcoholic beverages. However, in Maghreb, composed of the former French colonies of Tunesia, Algeria and Morroco, grapes used in France, such as Grenache and Cinsault, are grown and vinified. They even use the French AOC system – in Africa!

You should be hearing a lot more about South African wines, and perhaps other wines from this continent as well, into the future!

CHAPTER 14

OTHER COUNTRIES

While not having a major impact on the world of wine, at least currently, some specialty wines from other countries may come up in social discussions:

Greece

While international varietals are being used increasingly here, most grapes made into wine in Greece are native varieties, like the white Moscofilero (moe skoe fee leh row) and Savatiano (sa va tya no) and the red Agiorgitiko (ah yor yee ti ko) and Xnomavro (ksse no ma vro)

Greece's most famous wine is Retsina (ret cee nah), which actually accounts for 30% of this country's vinous output. It's made primarily from the Savatiano grape and is flavored with pine resin, a practice which is believed to have descended from the use of resin to seal the clay containers in which wine was stored in ancient times.

Hungary

The most famous wine of Hungary is Tokaji (toke uh ee), a sweet wine which has been affected by Botrytis. It is made from the local Furmint (foor mint) grape and has been most highly prized for centuries.

Uruguay

Tennat, which makes a bold red wine in southwestern France, has found a home here in South America.

LOOK OUT FOR – All countries in the Temperate Zone (roughly 30 to 50 degrees latitude) have the potential to make good wines. Larger countries, like China and Brazil, have an almost unlimited range of climates and *terroirs* in which the various wine grapes can rise to stardom.

As Steven and Maurice concluded in their slightly inebriated conversation at the conclusion of the movie *Bottle Shock*, the World is now ready for good wines from anywhere in the World!

CHAPTER 15

PAIRING FOOD AND WINE

Four things to remember about pairing food and wine, in descending order of importance, are:

1. Match the weight of the wine to the weight of the food.
2. Match the elements of the wine with the elements of the food.
3. Match the flavors of the wine with the flavors of the food.
4. If there is wine in the dish, serve that same wine with the meal.

First and foremost, match the weight of the wine to the weight of the food. If you are serving a heavy, winter-weather meal, serve a heavy winter-weather wine. If you have made something light and summery, serve a light, summery wine. This is where the old adage "white wine with white meat, red wine with red meat" really holds up. It is the quickest and easiest way to pair your food with wine.

Following is a list of meats from light to heavy along with a list of wines from light to heavy. This is a good, general guideline for pairing the weight of the food to the weight of the wine.

Food	Wine
White Shellfish	Albariño
White Fish	Riesling Chenin Blanc Pinot Gris
Pink Shellfish	Sauvignon Blanc
Fish Steak	Gewurztraminer Viognier
Chicken	Chardonnay
Turkey	Chardonnay Beaujolais
Lamb Chop	Beaujolais Pinot Noir
Sausage	Chianti
Beef and Pork	Cabernet Franc Tempranillo Merlot Zinfandel Syrah/Shiraz Cabernet Sauvignon Nebbiolo

There is a lot of overlap in these guidelines. Depending on how it is prepared, white fish with Chardonnay can be delightful, and Pinot Noir with turkey is becoming a Thanksgiving tradition. How the meat is prepared will in part determine which wine will pair best with the meal. If you're having a white fish with a heavy sauce, choose a wine that is a bit heavier. If you are having a white fish with lemon and olive oil, choose a lighter wine. But there are no circumstances in which Nebbiolo would ever pair with clams, nor could an Albariño ever stand up to any cut of beef.

Now, let's say you want to make a more sophisticated pairing, something beyond simply pairing the wine to the food by weight. That's when you go to rule number two. Match the elements of the wine with the elements of the food. The three elements of wine that you want to consider when pairing are acidity, sweetness and tannins. The elements of food that you want to consider are spiciness, saltiness, bitterness, umami (a savory taste, best exemplified in Asian dishes), sweetness and fats. Acidic wines work well with spicy, salty, fatty and umami foods. Tannic wines work well with fatty and salty foods and clash with spicy foods. Off-dry or slightly sweet wines work well with spicy and bitter foods. And sweet wines can work with sweet foods as long as the wine is sweeter than the food. The elemental pairings are depicted in short form below.

Sweet Food	Sweeter Wine
Desserts	Port, Marsala, Madeira, Some Sherries
Spicy and Bitter Food	Off-Dry Wine
Thai, Indian, Other Asian, Leafy Greens	Riesling, Chenin Blanc, Gewurztraminer
Spicy, Fatty, Salty, Umami Food	Acidic Wine
Asian, Mexican, Greens, Cheese, Meat	Riesling, Chenin Blanc, Pinot Noir, Chianti, Italian Reds, Cabernet Franc
Fatty and Salty Food	Tannic Wine
Pork, Beef	Merlot, Zinfandel, Syrah, Cabernet Sauvignon

But say you want to create a really special pairing, not just a pairing that enhances the elements of both the food and wine, but a pairing that seems to be greater than the sum of the parts. That takes us to the third step. Match the flavors of the wine with the flavors of the food. We've all done it at some point. We're sipping a wine, perhaps a new one we've never experienced before, and we notice a flavor or aroma that we've never perceived in any other wine. Maybe it's ginger, maybe it's almond, maybe we pick up on anise or bell pepper in a way that is certain and stunning. Remember that wine. The next time you serve it, pair it with a dish that uses one or a few of its aromas in the ingredients. It's really incredible when a wine matches up elementally with the food and also echoes the flavors of the meal.

Serve the wine with which you cook. If you're cooking with wine, make sure you have enough to serve with the meal. The longer the dish cooks with the wine, the more heavenly the experience that glass of wine will be.

CHAPTER 16

TASTING

Professional wine organizations, like the Court of Master Sommeliers and the Society of Wine Educators, conduct formal wine tastings. And they have participants evaluate wines, usually blind, on formal, multi-level rating scales. In such formal tastings, one is asked to go through "**The Four Ss**," which stand for **Swirl, Sniff, Savor and Spit**.

What we are preparing for here, however, is a much less formal kind of wine tasting, say at a friend's house when she casually asks you, "Well, Tom, what do you think of this Chardonnay?" or at a neighborhood wine shop where samples are given for marketing purposes.

Here you would swirl the glass to free up more of the aromas for smelling, but the swirling is done more subtly in such informal settings. You then smell the wine by inserting the tip of your nose into the bowl of the glass. Then take a little wine into your mouth and, after a step described immediately below, swallow the wine. So here "spit" becomes "swallow," spitting usually not being appropriate or even possible in such settings.

After taking a little of the wine into your mouth, we recommend the procedure put forward by another Wildman, Frederick this time. He suggests that you allow the wine to rest in the floor of your mouth. Then breathe in some air through your mouth and over the wine. Next, close your mouth and swallow the wine. Finally, exhale through your nose, which should give you a dramatic sampling of the olfactory qualities of the wine and, thus, reinforce your recent taste experience. It's a good idea to practice this procedure at home a few times before using it out in public. Coughing up wine is not likely to impress your clients, after all!

Almost always, as in the example above, you will know what kind of wine it is, either the varietal or the European appellation. We believe that the key to successful social wine tasting lies in the concept of "typicality." It is always, we think, appropriate to comment on the extent to which a wine is or is not "typical" of that kind of wine. Quite obviously, you need to know what to expect when you taste the main kinds of wines generally available today.

Accordingly, we are presenting below a little summary of what you would typically see, smell and taste when sampling different types of wines. Particularly prominent descriptors are underlined.

White Wines

Sauvignon Blanc. This is a <u>pale</u> wine in appearance. It gives off a lot of aroma, meaning that you can smell it some distance from the glass. It is <u>crisp</u> because it is an acidic grape. The hallmark smell and taste of a Sauvignon Blanc is <u>grass</u>. Those from Marlborough in New Zealand may also taste remarkably like <u>grapefruit</u> to which <u>tropical flavors</u>, like mango and passion fruit, have been added. Other aromas you might find in a Sauvignon Blanc are <u>melon</u> and <u>flint</u>. A Fumé Blanc, as discussed earlier, will tend to have a somewhat deeper taste because of its time in wood.

Pinot Grigio. This is also a <u>pale</u> wine like Sauvignon Blanc. However, it is <u>not so aromatic</u>, so you may suspect that you are being handed a glass of Sauvignon Blanc, but you won't smell the wine until your nose is almost to the glass. Pinot Grigios are, though, acidic and thus <u>crisp</u>. But they tend to lack the distinct grassiness and tropical fruit flavors of a Sauvignon Blanc. In fact, an official study program of the Society of Wine Educators described wines made from this grape as being "<u>refreshing but neutral</u>." They may also be <u>thin</u> and <u>vegital</u> (resembling the water in which vegetables have been boiled), as the grapes may be picked before ripeness as growers try to prevent the precipitous drop in acidy to which this grape is susceptible. An exception to this generally bland description of Pinot Grigios is in the French area of Alsace. It is called Pinot Gris here and may actually be described as "spicy." Other aromas experienced in both Pinot Gris and Grigio are <u>apple, lemon, peach and mineral</u>.

Riesling. The noble grape of Germany is also <u>pale</u> in color. And like Sauvignon Blanc, it is <u>aromatic</u>. It is characterized by what one expert calls "<u>soaring acidity</u>." This high acidity is sometimes balanced by <u>residual sugar, but not always</u>. But unlike Sauvignon Blanc, this is a <u>restrained</u> wine. Dry Rieslings are perhaps the most <u>elegant</u> wines in the world, displaying the kind of wholesome, simple and refreshing <u>minerality</u> one experiences in drinking from a cool, clean, rocky mountain stream. Fruit notes, such as those of peach and melon, are <u>restrained</u> in Rieslings. This grape is also said to have the quality of <u>transparency</u>, allowing the drinker to savor the qualities of the soils in which it was planted. Sweeter Rieslings have a <u>honey</u> quality about them. An almost infallible tip-off that you're being served a Riesling is that your glass will smell like gasoline! Fortunately, this <u>petrol</u> quality is not tasted when drinking.

Gewurztraminer. This is the signature grape of Alsace. This grape produces a wine that is high in alcohol but low in acidity, a combination which makes it feel <u>hot</u> in your mouth. Gewurz means "<u>spicy</u>" in German, so you won't be surprised to experience <u>curry-like flavors</u> when drinking this wine. Its tell-tale aroma is <u>ginger</u>.

Chenin Blanc, AKA Steen in South Africa. Chenin Blanc makes a <u>full-tasting</u> white wine which features a variety of fruit flavors, sometimes described as being a <u>fruit cocktail</u>. It has aromas of <u>apple, straw, melon, apricot, citrus and almond.</u> Its tell-tale aroma is <u>lanolin or wool</u>. It does not have a long finish, so it is usually considered to be a wine to quaff, as opposed to studiously savor, though its great acidity makes it a very food-friendly wine.

Albariño. This grape makes a <u>light</u> wine. It may have a <u>bit of effervescence</u>, perhaps because it is used in a region of Spain close to the part of Portugal in which the <u>spritzy</u> Vinho Verde is produced. Experienced tasters have reported both <u>lemon</u> and <u>spice</u> flavors when drinking this <u>frivolous</u> wine.

Chardonnay, AKA White Burgundy. As Chardonnay is the most planted and served white wine in the world, it may seem strange to cover it only at the end of the white grape section. The reason for this placement is that Chardonnay can present itself in radically different forms, depending on how it is treated in the winery. If it is fermented only once in stainless steel and not aged in oak, it will present as a <u>light, crisp</u> wine with a taste of <u>apple</u>, maybe even <u>green apple</u>. If, additionally, it undergoes a second, *malolactic fermentation*, it will take on a <u>creamy</u>, even <u>buttery</u> quality. Oak aging will add a <u>vanilla</u> taste and darken the wine. This oak aging can be taken too far, producing a wine that smells and tastes more like wood than fruit. Some vintners try to have "the best of both worlds" by treating Chardonnay grapes in different ways and then mixing the resulting batches together. Sometimes, but not always, this practice is successful in producing a wine that has a mouth-satisfying creaminess to it but still retains some crisp apple flavors. Chardonnays grown in cooler climates have more orchard fruit aromas such as <u>apple and pear</u>. But when grown in warmer climates, Chardonnays will present <u>tropical fruit</u> aromas.

Red Wines

Cabernet Sauvignon. This is, almost unquestionably, the most prestigious wine grape in the world. It makes a dark wine that smells of <u>anise</u> and <u>tobacco</u>. It is high in tannin, giving it a <u>mouth-drying</u> quality. Flavors detected in "Cabs" are dark, like <u>blackberry</u> and <u>black currant</u>. It may also give aromas of <u>eucalyptus, cedar and bell pepper</u>. It is often described as being <u>angular</u> and, particularly in its early years in the bottle, <u>abrasive</u>, both in tasting and during its long finish. This <u>lean, angular</u> characteristic is why it is so often blended with other red grapes, as in Bordeaux blends, and sneaked into the other 25% allowed in *California Cabs*.

Merlot. The grape most frequently used to <u>broaden</u> and <u>soften</u> Cabernet Sauvignon is Merlot. While Merlot has many of the same flavor characteristics as Cabernet Sauvignon, it is said to <u>fill out</u> the taste experience with <u>fruit jam</u> qualities.

Pinot Noir, AKA Burgundy. The classic Burgundian Pinot Noir is a <u>very light-colored red</u> wine. You could hardly be faulted for saying about a red wine through which you can see images, "Well, it certainly looks like a Pinot Noir to me." It will have an <u>earthy smell</u>, rather like the <u>floor of a forest</u>. It is more acidic than the other red noble grapes. A French Pinot Noir will taste less fruity than it smells, but you'll be delighted by a subtly-evolving <u>burnt cherry</u> taste in the <u>long finish</u>. A big, darker California "Pinot" allows you to remark how <u>atypical New World Pinot Noirs can be</u>.

Syrah, AKA Shiraz. This is a big red wine that often tastes of <u>spicy dark and damp cherries</u>. It can have aromas of <u>tar, leather, smoked meat, anise, rosemary, black pepper, lavender, earth and dried fruit</u>.

Petite Sirah. As discussed earlier, <u>Petite Sirah is an even bigger wine</u>, owing to the larger skin-to-juice ratio of its smaller grapes. It has <u>savory and dark fruit aromas</u>.

Gamay. This is the grape used to make Beaujolais. It is usually a <u>lighter red</u>. It <u>smells like flowers</u>, and its taste can strikingly resemble a diluted dish of <u>black cherry Jell-O</u>, particularly in Beaujolais Noveau. The process of carbonic maceration gives it <u>tropical fruit aromas</u>. It is a low alcohol, low tannin, medium acidity wine with a short finish.

Sangiovese. This is the principal grape in Chianti. It is a <u>lighter red</u> and, consistent with its taste, may have an <u>orange hue</u> to its color. Younger Sangioveses can be quite fruity, and a <u>hint of dried orange peel</u> in the taste is the "tell" for this wine. It often has a savory flavor and always has great acidity. Compared to the noble French grapes, this Italian native develops a wine <u>without a long finish</u>.

Tempranillo. As noted in the chapter on Spain, Tempranillo has <u>no distinct flavor profile</u>. However, these wines are increasingly being produced in fresher styles, and some tasters are reporting <u>red cherry</u> flavors in what in the past was a very woody wine. It will have less fruit aromas and more <u>leather and mineral</u> aromas.

Zinfandel. This is the US's (nearly) unique *vinifera* grape. It makes a <u>big, spicy</u> wine. Zinfandel gives away its identity when you <u>smell and/or taste pepper</u>. This pepper taste can be so strong that it <u>stings your tongue</u>, in fact! It has <u>dark fruit aromas</u> along with the pepper and other spices, such as <u>cinnamon and clove</u>. Zinfandel and Petite Sirah are two *vinifera* grapes that are grown more prevalently here in the United States than in their homes of origin. For that reason they are considered America's grapes.

We recommend that you make your tasting comments brief, humble and tentative, consistent with your current "junior" status. If anyone ever "accuses" you of being a "connoisseur" or "wine expert," vehemently deny it! Make some apparently self-depreciating comment like, "Oh, I just grew up around people who enjoy wines." Once again, your aim is to fit in, not to impress

Occasionally and despite your best efforts to avoid such situations, you may be asked to identify a wine blind. Approach this task tentatively, recalling the outline of what you experienced when tasting the wine and comparing it with what you've learned about the different grapes as summarized above, concluding with, "Well, it seems most like a _____ to me." Don't be embarrassed if you're wrong. Wine grapes are closely related, and we've heard experienced tasters make such comments as, "It's a _____, but it drinks like a _____." And look at the bright side – if your conclusion is reasonable, like not suggesting that a white wine is a Merlot, your failure will help you avoid being in any way threatening to your clients.

APPLYING YOUR WINE KNOWLEDGE

If you have read this work with any degree of conscientiousness, you now know more about wine than most people. Congratulations! But you must remember why you embarked on this project in the first place. It was definitely not to make you a know-it-all wine snob! As you will learn, the world has an elegant sufficiency of those! Besides, the last thing you want is for your affluent clients and corporate bosses to conclude, "Anne sure knows a lot about wine, but she's an insufferable bore about it." No, what you aim to do is convey subtly, perhaps "subliminally," the message, "We feel comfortable with her. She's one of us."

Assessing the Wine Knowledge of Others

Given that your goal here is fitting in, it's important to have an accurate assessment of the level of wine knowledge of the group into which you are attempting to blend. Here your status as a junior partner, associate or whatever is a definite plus. As a junior member of the group, you are expected to listen more than you speak. And as you are listening, you are both assessing their knowledge levels as well as learning.

Under learning, you are both acquiring more wine knowledge (at least usually!) and learning such things as how they pronounce wine terms. After all, are you better off pronouncing "Cabernet Sauvignon" like the sommelier in a Five-Star Paris restaurant or as the name of that grape is spoken by the Chairman of the Board? That's a rhetorical question, if you're keeping score!

There are, though, times when you'll need to make more active efforts at wine knowledge assessment. Let's say you're expected to entertain an important out-of-town visitor, which includes having her or him to your home for dinner one evening.

An advance call to the coming visitor would be a good first step here. This can be done under the guise of asking about her food preferences. Once a menu has been agreed upon, it would then be appropriate to ask what wine she prefers to have with that particular dish. You may get a number of responses here, all of which are potentially revealing:

1. "Oh, I'm sure anything you select will be fine for us." This, obviously, is an ambiguous response which reveals little. A probe or probes will be needed to achieve clarity here. You might suggest a wine and then ask if she likes that pairing and/or has other suggestions. If similar wines are proposed here, you are probably dealing with someone with rather extensive wine knowledge. Obviously, a lack of other suggestions here would indicate the opposite.

2. You sometimes get responses that might be characterized as being tangential. For example, let's say you're having some type of beef steak, and the reply to the wine question is, "My husband really likes Sauvignon Blanc." Obviously, this person doesn't know much about wine, to put it mildly! But how do you handle this situation when dinnertime comes? Our suggestion would

be to have the bottle of Sauvignon Blanc there, of course. Then you might say something like, "And if you'd prefer a red wine, we also have this Bordeaux, Cabernet Sauvignon, Malbec, etc."

3. If you get something like, "I've always liked a Bordeaux or a Napa Cabernet Sauvignon, but I'm becoming increasingly impressed with Argentinian Malbecs," you're dealing with a person with a great deal of wine knowledge. You also know that this is a kind person, in that usually Argentinian wines are good values for their price. You could never say that about French wines and California wines.

As is the case in so many areas of life, those who know a lot and those who know they know little are easy to entertain with wine. The problem is the person who doesn't know much about wine but thinks he does, or at least wants others to think he's an expert!

Buying Wine

An understanding of the level of wine knowledge of those with whom you will be socializing is essential to the successful and economical purchasing of wines for upcoming occasions. You see, people who know a lot about wine know that a good bottle of wine is not necessarily terribly expensive. This is not to say that an expensive bottle of wine did not cost more to make. There are costs to things like longer hang times, lower yields and new oak barrels. But a $200 bottle of wine, while it may be worth the price, will not necessarily taste 10 times better than a $20 bottle of wine. Putting all this together, for those who are ignorant about wines, you may need to buy a bottle that looks expensive!

For the more knowledgeable, however, you can afford to be more inventive. Let's say you're having a spicy meat dish, like a well-seasoned meatloaf. There's a California blend of "big'" grapes like Zinfandel and Petite Sirah which compliments such dishes beautifully. It's called "Kitchen Sink," presumably meaning that everything but the kitchen sink has been thrown in. And it's not very expensive, under ten dollars a bottle, as we recall. Someone who knows wines understands that U.S. wineries will often use self-depreciating, that is non-wine snob, names for their products. The Australians have raised this practice to an art form, with names like Molly Dooker and The Hattrick, both excellent wines. But someone less knowledgeable is likely to go back to New York and say something like, "Those rubes out in (Reno) served us this rot gut wine called, of all things, 'Kitchen Sink'!" Again, beware of "he who knows not but knows not that he knows not!"

A method that works for most levels of wine knowledge is to review the list of highly-rated wines at the back of the *Wine Spectator* each month. Certain vineyards in California, Oregon and Washington keep popping up there with some regularity. A good strategy involves looking for wines from those producers, like Robert Mondavi and Rutherford Hill. Of course, the wine you've actually purchased may not be the exact same wine so highly rated by the glossy magazine, but the label will give your guests some assurance that you have carefully chosen a good wine for their enjoyment. Besides, most wineries who make award-winning wines take such pride in their products that they simply won't release a bad wine under their label, so this strategy isn't merely window-dressing to impress.

Ordering Wine in Restaurants

If you are the host when with a group in a restaurant, you will be expected to order the wine, or at least make suggestions. Obviously, you should here follow the recommendations contained in the earlier wine-food pairing chapter.

When you order, the wine server will perform a little "ritual" with you. A small amount of the wine will be poured into your glass for your approval, and the cork will be placed to one side of your glass. Just look at the cork to ensure that it hasn't broken up, thus leaving bits of cork in the wine. Smelling the cork is an affectation. As one writer put it bluntly, "A cork should smell like a cork"! Assuming that the wine is not in some way "off," and very, very few are these days, signal your approval, and the server will fill the glasses of your guests, beginning with the ladies. Your glass will be the last to be completely filled.

Informal Wine Service

There are courses that teach sommelier candidates how to serve wine formally in elegant restaurants. They learn to do so standing at table side, keeping the label always visible to the host. Fortunately, the social service of wine involves fewer stiff contortions on your part!

In the practical, informal service of wine, there is no requirement that this be done in the presence of your guests, although you may do so if you wish, of course. Probably the easiest way to open a bottle is with a double lever corkscrew, which is very stable and gives you the most leverage. Leave both the corkscrew and the cork in the kitchen and present only the opened bottle to your guests.

You may at this point ask the most important guest if she or he would like to sample the wine to make sure it's a good pairing with the food. If she accepts that offer, pour her a goodly portion of the wine, say a quarter of a full serving, so she'll have something to work on as you fill the glasses of the other guests. Then pour the wine into the glasses of the other women and men present, complete the pour for the evening's VIP and then pour your own glass. Accomplish this process in a clockwise movement, if practical and possible in that dining room.

If there is no identified VIP or the offer to sample is declined, pour your own glass first, explaining, "I'll pour my glass first so I'll get any cork that may have split off," or something to that effect.

Glasses should be tulip-shaped and hold no less than a potential 12 ounces. Try to never pour a glass more than a third full. As a standard wine bottle holds 25 ounces, you will never get more than six servings from a bottle. So it's always wise to have another bottle of that wine on hand in case a guest or guests take a shine to that wine.

Opening a bottle of Champagne is about the only time in this area in which real physical danger may be possible. In fact, an ophthalmologist's wife had her eye put out when the doctor accidently let a cork fly. In the service portion of a sommelier examination, if you take your hand off the cork after the cage has been loosened (It takes six turns – count them.), you flunk – everything, no appeal. For most of us, it's best to perform this operation back in the kitchen, pointing the bottle's neck into a corner. Keep the non-dominant hand on the cork and cage and twist the bottle back and forth with the dominant hand. There should be only a gentle popping sound when the cork is finally removed, meaning no spilled bubbly.

Sparkling wines are the exception to the general rule that glasses should be filled in one continuous pour. For obvious reasons, you will need to keep "topping off" glasses of bubbly until they contain the desired amounts. Conventional wisdom to the contrary notwithstanding, the traditional Champagne flute is not ideal for bubbly as the narrowness of the lip doesn't allow the toasty aromas to collect and concentrate so you can appreciate them. The *Champagne Bowl,* supposedly molded from Marie Antoinette's left breast (closer to her heart, you see), is not the optimum vessel for sparkling wines either. The larger surface area allows the titillating bubbles to dissipate prematurely. It may not seem very romantic, but the old standard tulip-shaped glass is actually best for Champagne too.

Just for the sake of completeness, there's a totally different way to open sparkling wines. It's called *sabering.* You can even purchase special and expensive sabres from wine equipment supply houses. Using this method, you point the bottle away from you and with a glancing blow rap the neck with the sabre. If you're lucky, the neck will fly off, leaving some Champagne in the bottle for your guests. Too often, however, you're left with a lot of wine and glass on the ground. And even when it goes well, you still have to filter the wine to make sure no glass ends up in your guests' mouths. But despite all its problems, sabering is a wonderful way to really impress your superiors and colleagues, that is if you happen to work in a circus!

Storing Wine

Since at this point in your career you are still proving yourself, you're not expected to maintain an extensive underground wine cellar at what was considered room temperature in Eighteenth Century English manor houses. And the ambient temperature in modern apartments is too hot, and the fridge is too cold. What to do? For two or three hundred bucks you can buy a wine cooler that holds, say, 18 bottles of wine. Usually, there are two sections, one for white wines and one for red wines, which can be set at different temperatures. One of us keeps the wine cooler at the lowest possible settings, 50 degrees F for whites and 55 for the reds. These settings are a bit below recommended service temps, but the wines will, quite obviously, warm somewhat during the process of serving them. The presence of such a wine cooler in your home, additionally, will further boost your credentials as a member of the wine cognoscenti.

Tastings

In the earlier chapter on wine tasting we proposed a semi-formal method for identifying and evaluating wines. Going through a decision tree in a social setting would seem strange, probably show-offish. Talking through the formal grid of the Court of Master Sommeliers could get you committed!

We believe that the key to informal wine tasting relates to the issues of *typicality* and *atypicality*. It's always appropriate to make a comment to the effect that you sense the classic characteristics of a wine. A good example would be to remark that you can smell and/or taste the pepper in a Zinfandel. The big Pinot Noirs from Sonoma, on the other hand and in our opinion, justify a comment about how fruit-forward they are.

Some standard wine tasting comments we propose (when appropriate, of course) are:

Whites
    Sauvignon Blanc – Crisp
        New Zealand – Grapefruit, Grass
    Chardonnay –
        Un-oaked – Crisp apple
        Oaked – Buttery
    Riesling – Stunning acidity
    Viognier – Fruity and floral
    Chenin Blanc – Fruity and crisp

Reds
    Cabernet Sauvignon – "I can really smell the black currants and tobacco in this one!"
    Merlot – Typical Merlot jamminess
    Pinot Noir –
        Old World style – "This to me is a very European-style Pinot – delicate, elegant with subtle fruit at the end."
        New World Sonoma style – "Wow, it's very fruit forward!"
    Syrah/Shiraz – "You can really taste the cherry in this wine."
    Grenache – "You can feel the heat from the alcohol in this one."
    Sangiovese – "I see the slight orange tint to the wine and get the subtle taste of orange peel."
    Tempranillo – "Not a lot of fruit, but I sure taste the leather and mineral."
    Petite Sirah – "There's nothing petite about Petite Sirah."
    Zinfande - Pepper

Foreword from Here...

Recall that the purpose of your reading this book was to advance your career through giving you enough wine knowledge so you can blend in in social settings. Accordingly, you need to give some strategic thought to your next educational endeavor. It might develop that your best next step here should be to improve your golf game. Actually, it might be more in your interest to learn how to throw golf matches more convincingly! However, if you feel that there are still horizons in the wine world beckoning to you, and we hope you do, a study plan would be helpful to you. Of course, you're always welcome to reread this book!

For a more in-depth but not too time-consuming program of studies, Karen O'Neil's *The Wine Bible* and the 15-issues a year *Wine Spectator* magazine constitute a good plan of study. *The Wine Bible*, which is available through most major book stores, can be read by taking in a pair of pages on weekdays and four pages on weekends and holidays. The *Wine Spectator* publishes 40 to 50 pages a month, so you only have to read an average of less than two pages a day to read the issues cover-to-cover as they come out. *The Wine Bible* was published in 2001, so it gives a more traditional view of the wine world. The periodical *Wine Spectator*, on the other hand, tells you about up-and-coming trends in wine appreciation/studies.

Wine Spectator also offers a wonderful online series of wine classes that are interactive and will give you a good overview of the world of wine.

There are also live and video courses produced by The Society of Wine Educators and Court of Master Sommeliers. The Society of Wine Educators offers credentials relating to general wine knowledge, such as the Certified Specialist of Wine qualification. The Court of Master Sommeliers, on the other hand, focuses more on the intricacies of formal and elegant wine service. Its Master Sommelier level, which only 219 people in the world have achieved at the date of publication, is so valued that anyone with it can choose practically any city in the world in which to work and be guaranteed a well-paying job!

And, of course, there are also other books, such as Keven Zraly's *Windows on the World: Complete Wine Course,* Andrea Immer Robinson's *Great Wine Made Simple: Straight Talk from a Master Sommelier* and Oz Clark's *Let Me Tell You About Wine: A Beginner's Guide to Understanding and Enjoying Wine.* Many wine shops offer classes and tasting opportunities. And there is a wealth of information available at your local wineries, many of which offer tours and tastings. Take advantage of all of these occasions by listening and learning!

Regardless of where your professional career takes you, we wish you all success and happiness,

Linda and Bob

Printed in the United States
By Bookmasters